A CASE OF

MOTHER'S RUIN

Prelude to the Whitechapel murders

Martin Roberts

British Library Cataloguing in Publication Data.

A catalogue record for this book is available from the British Library

ISBN 978 0 86071 863 5

For Rufus and Alba
With love

A Commissioned Publication Printed by

MOORLEYS
Print, Design & Publishing
info@moorleys.co.uk · www.moorleys.co.uk

CONTENTS

ACKNOWLEDGEMENTS

Too many years have elapsed since I originally explored the potential relevance to the Whitechapel murders of the Gloster case; time permeated by sporadic further research, coupled with coincidental discoveries. Thanks are therefore long overdue to all those who facilitated my embarcation, travel, and arrival at this, my journey's end. Sadly I can no longer identify everyone by name. We have all moved on long since. Nevertheless, I trust those concerned would each recognize the role they played in my getting to this point, should they have occasion to read this account.

I must however acknowledge the invaluable past assistance of three correspondents in particular: Margaret McBride for Limerick Archives and Limerick Ancestry, Michael Bott at the University of Reading Library, and the late Nick Warren, Founding Editor of Ripperana magazine, who above all else deserves a posthumous 'thank you' for repeatedly demonstrating his breadth of knowledge, tireless enthusiasm, endless patience and equally unending encouragement. I hope this monograph does his memory justice.

Martin Roberts

Nottingham, England.

A Note on Sources

Readers wishing either to verify or discover further specifics pertaining to the Whitechapel murders of 1888 are referred to Philip Sugden's 'The Complete History of Jack the Ripper' and Paul Begg's 'Jack the Ripper - The Facts'. Both are excellent, detailed studies. The wealth of original correspondence connected with the case is comprehensively discussed by Stewart Evans and Keith Skinner in 'Jack the Ripper - Letters from Hell', whilst Evans & Gainey take credit for being the first seriously to broach the 'American' angle. Of the clutch of first-class accounts prompted by the centenary, those of Paul Begg, Donald Rumbelow, Martin Fido, Colin Wilson (jointly with Robin Odell) are all to be recommended. Needless to say there have been numerous contributions since.

With regard to this present examination, of Regina vs. Gloster in particular, the essential references are those appended to the author's original (1999) paper on the subject (Dr Who? Ripperana #30, 1-11). The case is also outlined by Peter Stubley in his book, '1888. London Murders in the Year of the Ripper' (2012). All witness statements quoted here have been transcribed from the case file previously kept at the Public Record Office, now the National Archive (CRIM 1/30/6 - Regina vs. Gloster (depositions)). Other details provided are thanks very largely to innumerable personal communications, UK census records, and the near infinite reach of a well-known internet search engine!

A Note as to Style

Quotes are occasionally italicised for emphasis - not a feature of the hand-written documents from which the words themselves derive.

PROLOGUE

A great deal has been written already about the Whitechapel murders of 1888, much of it detailing, in scholarly fashion, the crimes and the victims alike, and with the expectation as often as not that the killer's identity would be defined, not disguised, by the fog of contextual data. The late Stephen Knight, for instance, adopted this approach with his 'Final Solution', a hypothesis which eventually proved to be no solution at all, much less a final one. When your principal witness turns 'Queen's evidence' and publicly admits he made the whole thing up, as Joseph Sickert did, you know it's 'game over'.

Knight was neither the first nor the last to attach undue importance to the identity of those 'unfortunates' targeted by the Whitechapel murderer. Their significance as individuals was as wives, lovers, friends and family members, nothing more. As far as their respective fatal destinies were concerned, they simply had the misfortune to have been in the wrong place at the wrong time. Hence this present examination contains no victim-centric detail beyond a brief description of the circumstances in which their lifeless bodies were discovered.

A moment's thought with respect to communication in the Victorian age should make it quite clear that the Whitechapel murderer, whether acquainted with his victims or not, could not possibly have known exactly where they would be at night, unless by prior arrangement. Catherine Eddowes making her way to Mitre Square in the early hours of the morning from Bishopsgate police station, where she had been temporarily held for her own safety, i.e., to 'sober up', soon puts paid to that notion. Mary Kelly's is the one and only case of anything even approaching prior appointment.

Something else the reader will not encounter here is an attempt to 'fit up' a conspicuous, identifiable personality of the period, who just happened to be in London that autumn. There is no reference either to any long-lost relative or potentially relevant family heirloom.

On offer instead is simply an interpretation of certain evidence, and in a manner not previously attempted; evidence that will point in an altogether unexpected direction. Stephen Knight's 'Final Solution' included a chapter entitled, 'All Roads Lead to Dorset Street'. He was mistaken. The pathways point to Pennsylvania, via Pimlico, and the extraordinary case of a doctor who stood trial for murder at the Old Bailey during that same 'Autumn of Terror', as it came to be known.

Gin does indeed have a part to play in this story, although in what measure exactly remains unclear to this day. 'Ruination' in Victorian London was commonplace, as Hogarth had illustrated a century earlier, and Gin was, if not the culprit, the prime suspect. 'Bootlegging' was practised in London long before it featured alongside prohibition in 1920s America.

But the case we shall go on to explore has, at first glance at least, little to do with 'drabs' down on their luck in the poorer quarters of the Metropolis, although there *were* a great many of them. Instead it centres on an altogether different class of 'unfortunate'; one who could actually afford a dram or two. It also serves as a prelude to arguably the most horrific series of murders the civilised world has yet witnessed.

The passing of Eliza Schummacher in late June, 1888, quickly metamorphosed into the case of Regina vs. Dr James Gloster, largely on the strength of the poor woman's dying statement, which she made to Dr Crane, another attendant medical practitioner, who was called to the scene. There was undeniably 'bad blood' between the two parties of the first part. Unfortunately for Eliza it was hers that was shed, while the doctor under suspicion claimed he would have absolutely nothing to do with a patient whom he considered a 'bad drunken woman', reeking of gin.

As it turned out Eliza Schummacher's death was entirely unnecessary. The autumn of that year would herald the unnecessary deaths also of a handful of other women; inebriate habitués of London's Whitechapel district, for whom a 'tot' and an eventual 'ginny kidney'* were each attainable in life, whereas a doctor's 'guinea a visit' most certainly was not.

*The colloquial expression, 'ginny kidney', often encountered in discussions of the Whitechapel murders, is in fact clinically inaccurate. The late Nick Warren, surgeon and founder/editor of Ripperana, has put it thus: "There is no such thing as a 'ginny kidney.' In 1888 Bright's Disease was believed to be due to 'an overindulgence in ardent spirits,' but this is no longer the case."

CHAPTER 1

IN THE BEGINNING

In the eyes of some, the Metropolitan Police have of late acquired a rather unenviable reputation as regards their handling of case evidence. This should come as no surprise given events of a century and more ago, when a notorious precedent for impropriety in that same respect was set by the Commissioner himself!

It was very early in the morning of the 30th September 1888, immediately following *two* ghastly murders in London's East End, that Metropolitan Police Commissioner, Sir Charles Warren, saw fit to travel from Leman Street police station to nearby Goulston Street, where he would exercise his seniority over a discussion taking place there, at number 118/9.

Together with one or two of his Metropolitan Police colleagues, Sir Charles held counsel with members of the City Police over the immediate fate of some writing found chalked on the archway at the entrance to Wentworth Model Buildings. Earlier, at that same location, a blood-stained piece of apron had been retrieved from the tiled floor below by the Met's own patrolling police constable, Alfred Long, who had been the first to notice the written message in question at about 2.20 a.m. It was now getting on for 5.30.

The site of a most recent murder, with which these discoveries may well have been associated, actually lay within the jurisdiction of the City of London Police, but that did not stop Sir Charles from concurring with his own officers' opinion and over-riding their counterparts' preferred course of action (that the words remain *in situ* until daybreak, when they could be photographed). Warren was adamant the script be removed. The very glimpse of an unguarded reference to the Jewish population might spark a

1

riot, given the then tinder-dry political climate of the capital, or so Superintendent Arnold had suggested, and Warren averred.

Accordingly Warren, Arnold, and the various constables in attendance at the time, all collaborated, actively or otherwise, in the destruction of evidence; an action the City of London Police Commissioner, Major Henry Smith, would later describe as 'a grave mistake'. It was a pivotal moment in the hunt for the Whitechapel murderer, 'Jack the Ripper', as the press had already dubbed him.

Warren's actions were consistent with those of an ex-army officer unaccustomed to being upstaged by subordinates. The killer of two that very night and presumed author of the Goulston Street graffito, as it has since come to be known, had been leading the 'Met' a merry dance for a month, since launching his assault on downtrodden female members of society early in the morning of the 31st August, when it is generally supposed the first of his unsuspecting victims succumbed to his plausible charm. Hardly a week elapsed before another followed suit. September's end had now brought the sacrificial total seemingly to four.

The police had so far questioned all and sundry, but charged no one. Small wonder therefore that frustration was beginning to show.

*

Frustration had not been the reason for Mary Ann (aka 'Polly') Nichols to walk the streets in the early hours a month earlier. She was not simply in need of some night air. On that last day in August, equipped with a 'pretty new bonnet', she was off to earn her doss money - the four pence it would take to secure a bed in one of Whitechapel's plentiful lodging houses.

Somewhat less than sober, she chose, on this occasion, to ply her trade along Buck's Row, where she would proceed to strike her very last bargain for sexual concourse, while standing in front of a pair of large gates nearby to Kearley and Tonge's warehouse. That is where two men on their way to work would afterwards encounter her prostrate body, Charles Cross at 3.45 a.m., Robert Paul a minute or two later. A passing constable (PC Neil) would confirm Nichols' murder after both men had already set off in the opposite direction – in search of a policeman! However, it was not until Polly's corpse was examined at the mortuary that the extent of her injuries became clear.

Quite apart from having had her throat cut, her abdomen was savagely torn open, from her genitals to her breast bone, an atrocity that initially went unnoticed in the dim street light, on account of Polly's 'stays' and her long coat, which had also absorbed much of her blood.

Murder in the densely populated capital was by no means a novelty in Victorian England. In the wider context of the age therefore, whether the victim of an unduly optimistic thief, a drunken husband or vengeful rival, Polly Nichols would soon have become little more than a crime statistic, but for what happened the following week.

Forty-seven-year-old Annie Chapman, known to some as 'Sievey' or 'Sivvey', was another lady constantly teetering on the brink of personal socio-economic disaster, as were so many of the period. She might be selling violets one day, her body the next, doing whatever it took to survive. Getting into a fight with a fellow lodger over a bar of soap is a fairly clear indication of the levels of desperation to which she and her contemporaries were driven.

Annie too was out and about early on the morning of the 8th September. She failed to live out the day. Instead her lifeless body was first noticed shortly after 5.45 a.m., lying between the back steps and the boundary fence at number 29 Hanbury Street. The dubious honour of discovery fell to John Davis, one of seventeen residents at the address. Another, John Richardson, who had sat on those very steps barely an hour earlier in order to trim some redundant leather from a boot, had seen nothing out of the ordinary, but Davis' unwelcome experience would shake him to the core.

Annie was almost decapitated, such was the force with which her throat had been cut. Her legs were splayed apart, her skirts raised up and her abdomen again torn open, exposing her intestines, part of which had been placed across her right shoulder, other flesh just above her left. Her uterus had been completely removed.

It was this gory scene that confirmed in an instant the presence and activity in Whitechapel of a determinedly savage killer. Polly Nichols had opened the ball it seemed. There could well be more fatal dances to follow. And so it transpired.

The 'double event', so called, is the popular nomenclature used to refer to the murders of two more Whitechapel 'unfortunates', both committed in the early hours of the 30th September, the occasion of Sir Charles Warren's one and only expedition into the area; drawn, not to either crime scene, but the site of that one handwritten sentence and piece of bloodstained cloth.

'Long Liz' Stride was the first to die. She was eventually encountered just after 1.00 a.m. by luckless trader Louis Diemschutz, whose pony shied away from stepping on her still warm body, as man, horse, and cart struggled to enter the yard immediately behind the Jewish club in Berner Street.

Liz had not suffered the same grotesque mutilations as those victims before her, although her throat *had* been similarly cut across. She lay on her back with a red carnation still in her lapel and her blood draining away into the gutter.

Just three quarters of an hour later the cry of 'Murder!' went up again, this time emanating from a dark, unlit corner of Mitre Square, situated on the opposite side of Aldgate High Street. If any doubts attended authorship of Elizabeth Stride's demise, there could be no question that Catherine Eddowes' condition was the Whitechapel ghoul's handiwork.

Described (to a *Star* journalist) by PC Watkins, who discovered the body, as 'ripped up like a pig in a market', Catherine Eddowes had been subjected to an extraordinary level of abuse by her assailant. Quite apart from an array of internal injuries very similar to those inflicted upon Annie Chapman, Eddowes' face had been mutilated, her nose cut off, her eyelids cut through and triangular flaps cut into her cheeks.

Those who shared PC Watkins' distress at seeing the body of Eddowes *in situ* could scarcely believe the level of degradation they witnessed. Unbelievably almost, worse was to follow, although it took over a month to happen.

On the morning of the 9th November, the day of the Lord Mayor's parade, Thomas Bowyer (aka 'Indian Harry') called at number 13 Miller's Court on behalf of local landlord John McCarthy, to collect overdue rent from McCarthy's beleaguered tenant, Mary Jane Kelly. It was a routine call he would afterwards regret having made.

At 25, 'Marie Jeanette', as she styled herself, was considerably younger than Nichols, Chapman, Stride or Eddowes, and still endowed with sexual allure. While she may not have entirely welcomed her situation in life, she seemed perfectly accustomed to being a kept woman. She also had a sympathetic disposition, despite being thought of as having something of a temper when in drink, a trait not out of keeping with her presumed Irish parentage. It was this streak of kindliness which was to prove her undoing.

Along with no doubt every other female resident of the district, Mary Kelly was fearful of the Whitechapel murderer. She even had her live-in lover, Joseph Barnett, read her the news reports of the day. How strange then, that very early on that fateful morning Mary Jane should inexplicably throw caution to the wind. Perhaps it had something to do with Barnett's no longer being on hand to offer advice, having reluctantly abandoned her to her own devices when she persisted in allowing others to share their scant accommodation.

An unscripted meeting on the street with a 'gentleman' led to Mary's being offered the use of a red silk handkerchief on the spur of the moment, and the gentleman's being invited to stay the night in return. Wearing a frock-coat trimmed with Astrakhan, white spats, a gold watch and a horseshoe tie-pin, he appeared beyond reproach – except, that is, to observant bystander George Hutchinson, who thought him suspicious.

Long after the Whitechapel murders had ceased, a study of beat officers' reports led to the conclusion that the Whitechapel killer was 'not one of the ordinary denizens of that place'. Mary Kelly's unexpected, and most probably last, nocturnal guest was certainly a 'cut above' in terms of his wardrobe. The word 'cut' however is scarcely adequate to describe the apparition which greeted poor Thomas Bowyer when he failed to elicit a response by knocking at the door.

Desirous of moving on to his next call, Bowyer took the liberty of passing his hand through a broken window pane so as to draw aside the piece of sack cloth which served as a curtain. He immediately wished he had not.

The interior of Mary Jane Kelly's one-room lodging had all the appearances of a butcher's shambles. What remained of her body lay on the bed against the far wall opposite the window. Her limbs had been flensed, her face hacked about, her breasts cut off and placed on a small table adjacent. Ironically almost, the *post mortem* accounted for all her internal organs save her heart, which had quite possibly been cast onto the open fire, since this had burnt overnight with either ferocity or persistence enough to melt the spout from a copper kettle standing in the hearth.

It was the bloodiest of grand finales. Nothing like it was experienced in Whitechapel, or anywhere else in London, subsequently. Assistant Chief Constable of the 'Met', Sir Melville Macnaghten, would report that 'the Whitechapel fiend had five victims, and five victims only'.

*

Set against this most bestial of backdrops, the incidental discovery of a piece of cloth, coupled with a few lines of doggerel, seems scarcely worth more by way of commentary than a metaphorical column inch, which is what most authors on the subject tend to give it, while supposing Sir Charles Warren's editorial decision to have been justified. Superficially, the script, as commonly understood, does indeed have the appearance of an anti-semitic jibe and might well have been seen as a fuse in a powder-keg at the time (the Arnold-Warren interpretation). It was nevertheless a clue of sorts, and in relation to a very real murder, not a hypothetical situation. It should have been preserved.

Although Sir Charles cannot be accused of striking the message from the record altogether (since he personally kept a copy of it, as did the men on duty), all that remain to us are the words themselves. We have nothing of their true visual context and, for all we know, what the writing actually looked like might have conveyed a good deal more than simply what was said, just as it might well have informed Warren, whose eventual justification of his actions that morning was disingenuous. So what exactly did it say?

Arranged in accordance with its scansion, as recognised in a memo from Sir Charles Warren to under Secretary of State, Godfrey Lushington, the Goulston Street graffito read as follows:

> The Juwes are
> The men That
> Will not
> be Blamed
> for nothing

Bearing in mind that the message was written within the narrow margin of a brick archway, no more than about a foot wide, one might look to dismiss the line-breaks for that reason alone, but it is worth paying attention to the scale of the piece overall. As well as being written in a 'good schoolboy hand', according to PC Long, the capital height was no more than about ¾ of an inch, with lower-case letters in proportion.

Suddenly, this supposed exhortation to riot seems rather more in keeping with the author's saying something *about* Juwes in particular than his aiming a provocative taunt *at* Jews in general. But wouldn't someone desirous of inciting a riot among selective members of the population at least have taken the trouble to spell their collective identity correctly?

CHAPTER 2

RETRIBUTION, IN OTHER WORDS

At the inquest into the death of Catherine Eddowes, the City solicitor, Mr Crawford, was careful to establish the spelling of the word 'Juwes', as transcribed by Detective Halse of the City of London Police. It has assumed a mantle of mystery ever since.

As a variant of the word 'Jew' it is positively archaic and would have been so in Victorian England even. For author Stephen Knight, as obsessed with unmasking Freemasonry as he was receptive to Joseph Sickert's little fantasy (woven around Prince Albert Victor's secret catholic wedding, a blackmail attempt, followed by 'cloak-and-dagger' reprisals on behalf of the establishment), 'Juwes' represented three treacherous characters of Masonic antiquity (Jubelo, Jubela and Jubelum), a trio of craft masons, who conspired to murder their master, Hiram Abif, the architect of Solomon's temple. Knight's interpretation of the 1888 scenes of crime in Whitechapel was that they graphically reflected the punishment eventually meted out to these three felons by order of the disgruntled king.

Stephen Knight's 'Juwes' theory proved so persuasive, at least until Sickert pulled the plug on his own deceit, that those addressing themselves to the subject since have found it as difficult to shake off as Ridley Scott's 'Alien'. Despite countless man-hours of research, the conclusion appears to be, as others have previously stated, that 'Juwes' is not, and never has been, a Masonic word.

In point of fact, the particular episode of Masonic folklore to which the word 'Juwes' was supposedly related had been dropped from the workings of the Craft in England a century before, although it persisted in America, where the three protagonists are identified collectively, even today, as either 'the ruffians' or 'the three hanged men'. One must always be careful not to throw the baby out with the bath water however. In this case 'dropped from the workings' might be better viewed as 'relegated to the substitute's bench' rather than 'unavailable for selection'.

Christopher Knight and Robert Lomas, both Freemasons (admitted 1976, 1986 respectively), make explicit reference to 'the Juwes' in their own study of the Masonic order, 'The Hiram Key' (1996):

> ...a past Master gave an explanation of the Third Degree. The three villains who murdered Hiram Abif were identified as Jubela, Jubelo and Jubelum, known jointly as the Juwes; pronounced Joo-ees.

Rushing to espouse the idea of a Masonic connection with the Whitechapel murders on this basis alone would be impetuous. However, there are, as we shall see, grounds for suspecting a hidden connection between the killer and his pursuers, though not perhaps for the 'royal conspiracy' reasons hitherto advanced by Stephen Knight.

A keen archaeologist, and sometime director of excavations in Palestine, Sir Charles Warren was himself one of the UK's leading Freemasons, having founded the Quatuor Coronati lodge of Masonic research in 1886. He was both a classical scholar and military engineer, rising to the rank of General before accepting the position of Commissioner of the Metropolitan Police, again in 1886.

It is fitting we take Warren's grammar school education into account when considering what he had to say to Under Secretary of State, Godfrey Lushington, about his decision to erase the chalked writing at Goulston Street, allied to his interpretation of the word 'Juwes'. He wrote on the 11th October:

Dear Mr Lushington,

I send you a copy of the writing on the wall at Goulston St. The idiom does not appear to me to be either English French or German but it might possibly be that of an Irishman speaking a foreign language. It seems to be the idiom of Spain or Italy.

The spelling of Jews or Jewes is curious.

truly yours

CW

What makes this advice of Warren's disingenuous, if not suspicious, is that, as a former Grammar School boy, he should have known the letter 'w' does not appear in the Latin alphabet. Consequently it plays no role either in derivative European languages, e.g., Italian or Spanish. Notice too, that despite affixing an accurate transcript, Warren subtly reaffirms his *public* interpretation of it by referring to 'Jews' or 'Jewes' within his covering letter.

This interpretation of Warren's, coupled with the possibility that the writing as a whole might have borne some pictorial significance (implicit in the irregular use of capital letters, say), suggests Freemasonry might have been a point of reference after all. Since Sir Charles Warren saw fit to obliterate the original, and thereby prohibit any subsequent imaging of it, we may never know the answers to such questions.

Whoever the 'Juwes' may have been, the Goulston Street author possibly viewed himself as one of them, in which case he would not have been referring to three long-since-mummified residents of the Middle-East, writing as he did in the present tense. Nevertheless, the idea of 'threeness' may yet prove pertinent.

As previously noted, Sir Charles Warren expressed the opinion, at least once, that the writing on the Goulston Street wall was indicative of an Irish author toying with a foreign idiom. However, the Goulston Street graffito was not written in cuneiform, hieroglyphics, or Gaelic even, but in plain English. The only real oddity, if such it may be called, was that which Warren described as a 'curious spelling'.

Hence his questioning of 'the idiom' must apply largely, if not entirely, to the word 'Juwes', which he then decided was not representative of English, French or German, but somehow of an Irishman attempting to speak a foreign language, i.e., *not* English, but not French or German either. Somewhat unhelpfully, from Lushington's point of view, Warren inappropriately went on to suggest Spanish or Italian as a potential context for understanding.

Where in all of this is there any indication that said author was Irish? Did Sir Charles Warren see something on the wall early that morning, which, for obvious reasons, we cannot, or did he simply succumb to the music hall cliché of an Irishman, supposing the writer to have 'spelt it like it sounded', but in Spanish for effect? In the absence of any truly recognisable hint of Irishness, Warren's comment would turn out to be eerily prescient, as we shall go on to discover.

Historians and others have generally taken the Goulston Street missive to suggest a disgruntled anti-Semite, immune to the logical significance of the 'double negative'; a cockney with a chip on his shoulder perhaps. If, however, the scribe's intention had been to declare that 'Jews won't accept the blame for anything they do wrong', then why did he not simply say so? On the contrary, instead of referring to the Jews as a whole, he appears to have singled out an exclusively male sub-set of the population (the 'Juwes') as being '*the* men', specifically, 'who will not be blamed for nothing'.

Taken at face value this is not a grammatical corruption at all, but a hint that the 'Juwes' (including the writer, should he have considered himself one such) were of a mind to get their own back, i.e., to be 'hung for a sheep', if being hung for a lamb were already in prospect. (Remember the 'three hanged men'?)

Without subscribing to occult symbolism, dialectic variation, or the misrepresentation of foreign languages, it is perfectly possible to read the Goulston Street message as referring to an earlier misdemeanour of which the author had already been considered guilty.

Apart from proximity in the doorway to the piece of blood-stained apron, which subsequent perusal confirmed had been cut from that worn by Catherine Eddowes, there is nothing to establish that the writing was in any way connected with the recent spate of murders. On the other hand, PC Long's beat took him past no. 118 twice that morning, yet he only noticed the items, both of them, on the second occasion. If they appeared together, then there was every chance they belonged together.

Thus there is some justification at least for supposing Catherine Eddowes' killer and the anonymous Goulston Street scribe to have been one and the same. If that were the case, whatever the foregoing misdemeanour over which he seems to have taken umbrage it will have been at least as serious as the vengeful course on which he was presently embarked. Furthermore, given the media's appetite for shocking news, it is likely to have been reported. It would also have been fairly recent, since already executed felons are no longer capable of personally exacting revenge. Murder was a capital offence in Victorian England and there was no court of appeal.

*

A number of murder cases did indeed pass through the courts in 1888 prior to the 'Autumn of Terror', the most intriguing, for present purposes, being that of Regina vs. Gloster.

The Gloster in question was a doctor of medicine, qualified also in surgery and midwifery, who stood accused of conducting an unlawful operation upon one Eliza Schummacher, a lady patient who believed herself to be pregnant at the time. Mrs Schummacher unfortunately died as a result and, largely owing to her dying declaration, written down by fellow physician Dr Crane, Dr Gloster was charged with murder. Things become even more intriguing once it is discovered that Dr James Cockburn Gloster was Irish, from Limerick, and whose family home in Rockfield, Ballynacarraga was just a few miles from what some have reckoned to be the birthplace of Mary Jane Kelly.

In view of what occurred during the Autumn of Terror, Regina vs. Gloster has more than an air of relevant mystery about it. Witness depositions across the board posed as many questions as they yielded answers, whilst the very nature of the case appears puzzling. Dr James Gloster stood accused of performing a haphazard operation upon his patient in an attempt to abort a pregnancy when his patient was not in fact pregnant.

Would someone qualified in midwifery, medicine and surgery have first arrived at a mistaken diagnosis, then gone on to perform a careless and unnecessary operation into the bargain? Was Eliza Jane Schummacher really the hapless victim she presented herself as being, or were darker motives involved?

These and other questions invite a detailed examination of proceedings in this particular case, as Regina vs. Gloster may well have been the reason why Regina vs. 'Jack the Ripper' was never brought to court.

Accordingly, what now follows is a full account of the Gloster trial; an event in which the seeds of the Whitechapel murders may very well reside. It is a little known case with far reaching implications. Witnesses are quoted verbatim from their own depositions or answers given in court, as the affair progressed from the July inquest into the victim's death, through the Magistrate's court on the 17th, and ultimately to the Old Bailey two months later, where a final verdict was reached, but under such extraordinary circumstances as to warrant a closer examination of the evidence than was eventually permitted at the time.

CHAPTER 3

THE INITIAL INCISION

By the standards of the age (1888) Eliza Schummacher was not a remarkable woman. Thirty-nine years old, with a young son (although bereaved of another six years earlier), she was four or five years separated from her husband, a 'gentleman's servant', yet nevertheless enjoyed the privilege of living in a rather pleasant part of the capital. Districts wax and wane in popularity over time, but Moreton Place, Pimlico was, and remains, a fashionable area, situated in what contemporary estate agents describe as the 'Moreton Triangle'.

Over a seven year period, Mrs Eliza Schummacher occupied a number of different addresses in Moreton Place (nos. 47, 49 and 24), before settling at no. 21, a substantial dwelling, arranged on several stories and part of a respectable Georgian terrace, replete with classical pediments, that still features the gold stock brick typical of those earlier, more up-market inner-London developments. If sold today the house would command a price in excess of £2 million.

Besides receiving a modest allowance from her estranged husband, Mrs Schummacher was something of a business woman. Her residence was also her workshop, from which she operated as a dress and mantle maker. She had several female lodgers and a number of employees serving different functions, such as sewing and finishing; even letter writing. She did not operate a deficit and could afford the occasional bottle of spirit. When the necessity arose she could also afford the private attentions of a doctor (a guinea a visit was the going rate). Eliza Schummacher was therefore a solvent and, by all accounts (those of her sisters at least), a sober woman.

But the lot of the small trader is a precarious one. Eliza had frequently to be 'out and about' with clients, for once in motion an operation such as hers had to be sustained. There was no fall-back position, and allowances go only so far after all. Unplanned interruptions in the shape of indisposition were the stuff of nightmares and, in April of that year, Eliza may well have experienced one. In May she genuinely believed it to be coming true and feared ruin would result. That well-worn cliché, 'what am I to do?' was uppermost in her mind if not audibly on her lips, although it very soon would be.

Eliza was on good terms with her various sisters, one of whom, Mrs Emily Maud Baker, visited fairly regularly, and it was Emily Maud, that spring, in whom Eliza first confided she was pregnant. There seemed nothing questionable therefore about Eliza's inviting her to call on the 8th June, when they went shopping together. After which, and with Eliza complaining of a pain in her back, they paid a more unusual visit, to 22 Wardour Street and a Doctor Louis Tarrico. Dr Tarrico first examined Eliza (although not in her sister's presence) then gave her a prescription – for rhubarb pills! He was unable to confirm that the patient was 'in the family way' as she supposed, but suggested she could return to see him, if she wished, between 8 and 9 p.m. on any night.

Eventually the sisters adjourned to 'Stagg and Mantles' store, from which they afterwards made their uneventful way home. Parting company with Emily Maud at the end of the street, Eliza walked unassisted to her door. She appeared in rude health the following week, when Emily Maud again responded to an invitation to visit, on Saturday the 16th. This visit was a brief one however, Emily Maud leaving Eliza to her morning's work shortly before 11 a.m. - 48 hours later and things would be altogether different.

From being merely uncomfortable following a seemingly routine medical examination, Eliza Schummacher was now, the

18th June, lying ill in bed. She sent her 'improver', the sixteen-year-old Miss Barnes, to fetch her sister Emily once more. Dutifully, Emily appeared shortly after 4 p.m., when she was surprised to discover the ailing Eliza prostrate in bed in the back room on the ground floor, complaining of pain in her bowel, and with a small bottle of medicine for company. She remained until midnight.

Matters progressed swiftly, from bad to worse. Emily returned to her sister at a quarter to six the next morning, Tuesday 19th, and stayed until eight. She returned again after breakfast, then went home to dinner, returning once more at 3.30 p.m. Eliza was still in bed, but Emily remained with her all night, noting that she slept a little towards morning ("I gave her some tea and a hot bath. She was very sick.").

The following morning, Wednesday 20th, Eliza was much worse and, despite not having a regular 'medical man', encouraged Emily to seek out a Dr Gloster, whose practice was in nearby Kensington. This she did, before 11 a.m., but Dr Gloster declined to attend, suggesting instead that Emily visit Dr Tarrico once more on her sister's behalf and invite *him* to make a house call – at a cost of *two* guineas. On receipt of this information however, Eliza did not encourage her concerned sister to pursue the recommendation.

Without medical attention of any kind for a further 48 hours, Eliza's condition worsened, to the point where Emily, no doubt distressed at her sister's circumstances, urged her to call in a doctor - any doctor. Reluctantly almost, Eliza finally demurred, whereupon Emily set off to enlist the help of a local man, Dr Albert Crane, whom she knew personally. Dr Crane appeared shortly before 2 p.m. and, following a conversation with his new patient, called in a colleague, Dr William Frankish of Sloane Street. It was now Friday, the 22nd June.

Despite Dr Crane's conscientious ministrations, Eliza's condition worsened, such that she complained every day of her suffering and, on the Wednesday following, told Emily, quite unequivocally, that she 'never expected to get up again' and that Dr Gloster, who had declined to attend at the house when Emily sought him out, had 'torn her insides to pieces'. Eliza Schummacher died that same night, but not before giving a detailed statement to Dr Crane, in the presence also of Dr Frankish and the distraught Emily.

The devil, as they say, is in the detail. The following is what Eliza Schummacher confided to Doctor Crane, who, when he heard it, no doubt felt he had himself picked up a poisoned chalice:

ELIZA SCHUMMACHER'S DYING DECLARATION

My name is Eliza Schummacher. I am living apart from my husband. I thought I was pregnant and I went to see Dr Gloster at 15 Upper Phillimore Place. He said as I had mentioned the subject for which I had gone to him he could not have anything to do with me. I had mentioned it to a gentleman at Dr Gloster's who sometimes assisted him. Now he said go to Dr Tarrico. I wanted him to write the address and he said no – no one can mistake a memo like this. He told me to ask Dr Tarrico if he would examine me for something for the womb and if Dr Tarrico did so examine me then he, Dr Gloster, would take on the case.

Then I went to Dr Tarrico and he passed an instrument, that was on the same day, in the evening, as I went to Dr Gloster. That was last Thursday four weeks. Dr Tarrico did not hurt me, he was gentle. I went to Dr Gloster next day and he passed an instrument into my body which hurt me very much. He came to see me here on the 11th June and he again passed an instrument which hurt me very much. I have been in pain ever since and unable to get up. He said if I was very bad I was to send for him. I did send for him. I was in great agony.

I cursed him.

He did not pass an instrument that day. He brought some medicine. He applied some cotton wool saying it will stop the pain. I thought he had left the cotton wool inside me. I did not see him again. I have never been well since and I do not think I am going to be so. I make this statement with the fear of death before my eyes.

(signed) Eliza Schummacher

Witness, Charles Albert Crane M.D.

W.J. Frankish. L.R.C.P. Lon. & c.

June 27 1888

Eliza Schummacher had clearly taken what would ultimately prove to be a fatal decision. She had approached various members of the medical profession with a rather naïve request for assistance; naïve, since the help she actively sought would entail a doctor's contravening the then current statutes, consequently putting their own liberty in jeopardy, never mind their livelihood. (Against such a social backdrop, the rise of the 'back-street operative' should be perfectly understandable.)

The odds were therefore against Eliza emerging physically unscathed from the treatment she entreated of others. Unbeknown to the patient however, salvation was potentially at hand – she was not even pregnant. So what went wrong? When did it happen? And who really was responsible?

CHAPTER 4

CONFLICTING OPINIONS

As cut-and-dried as the Schummacher case may have appeared
initially, it very soon proved to be anything but. The seemingly
close professional association between Dr James Cockburn
Gloster, of 15 Upper Phillimore Place, Kensington and Dr Louis
Tarrico, 'accoucheur', of 22 Wardour Street, Piccadilly, was the
first 'slippery eel' to be examined, and the first to slide from the
grasp. No sooner had Eliza Schummacher identified the players
involved than Dr Gloster set about moving the goalposts.

From Inspector Burner's initial account of the arrest we learn
that Dr Gloster said of the deceased:

> Her sister came to me and said that her sister
> was in a certain way. I sent her to another
> Doctor and he attended her.

The other doctor is not identified here, but one might
immediately question how Dr Gloster was able to conclude 'he
attended her' solely on the strength of his own recommendation.
Nevertheless, those present at the Coroner's Court had the
benefit of Emily Maud Baker's first-hand account of *her* meeting
with Dr Gloster.

> I asked him what I should do if my sister was to
> die. He said I was to go back and tell her to send
> for Dr Tarrico.

And that observation put Dr Louis Tarrico squarely, and
uniquely, in the frame. Unbeknown to Dr Gloster however, Louis

Tarrico, despite his poor command of English, had managed to give a somewhat fuller account of their relationship, thanks to the intervention of an Italian speaker, Sergeant Edward Clough:

> Dr Gloster came to me, I do not know the date, 8 or 10 days ago about. He said 'I have a friend, a patient', he said he wished to see her with me. I said, 'Very well, I don't object.' He said it is a congestion or an ulceration of the womb.' I said, 'Very well.' He came the day after, and he came first, and after he went downstairs he brought a lady upstairs to my front room. I said 'What is the matter?' She said, 'I do not know' and she said if to examine her not to be hurting. She was to have chloroform. I said I am not used to hurt my patients and it was not necessary at all.
>
> I examined her by finger and said I do not know what it is. Perhaps it might be congestion. I said 'If you have anything you must attend and wait. You must use a hip bath and what Dr Gloster will give to you.' Then Dr Gloster asked me, 'What is your opinion?' I said, 'It was not very easy to know.'
>
> He went away with the patient and I have not seen him anymore. He asked me about my fee and I said, 'Not anything.' I laughed then. I have known him about 4 or 5 years since he took the business on and sent me customers. I had some of his cards but I cannot find them. I have made no entry in my book for some time.

Although given partly in Italian and partly in English, this statement of Dr Louis Tarrico's, as recorded by Sergeant Clough, makes it abundantly clear that the business relationship between himself and Doctor James Gloster of West Kensington was by no means one of happenstance, but of several years standing.

There is camaraderie within any profession of course, but inevitably, given the medical mores of the period, the readiness of a socially elevated surgeon, trained in midwifery, to 'send customers' to an unregistered male midwife in Soho, might prompt a raised eyebrow or two at the very least.

Dr Gloster, it appears, was not totally forthcoming with his initial description of patient referral, although, to be fair, a measure of reticence is to be expected of early witness testimonies, masking an understandable reluctance to answer questions which have yet to be put. The term 'confused declaration' is one of general pertinence to this case however, since, as will eventually become apparent, it epitomises the accounts of prosecution and defence witnesses alike. Dr Gloster's was not the only eel in the barrel here and maintaining a grasp of the truth would be far from easy.

Nevertheless, it was decided by the magistrate at Ebury Bridge that the doctor had a case to answer and he was held on remand, pending his trial for murder at the Old Bailey, where his defence counsel would see to it that their affluent client (who proceeded to stump up £450 bail without demur – a *very* considerable sum at the time) would certainly get his money's worth. Opposing Mr Poland (prosecuting for the Crown), Dr Gloster's Irish compatriot, Mr Gill, was a smooth operator if ever there were; one who more than lived up to the title 'Silk'.

For the present, however, we should give a little more attention to the medical facts of the matter.

Doctors Crane and Frankish, who were both present at the autopsy, could not disagree with what their colleague, Dr Bond, encountered and described. Poor Eliza Schummacher's uterus had been perforated by the seemingly careless use of a diagnostic tool; a probe intended for examination, not incision. The wound was therefore brutal, and whoever caused it attempted to staunch the lesion by inserting cotton wool at a location to which it could not otherwise have found its way. That is where Dr Bond discovered it. The wound was not dressed, but plugged, and it subsequently festered.

An entirely reasonable point in favour of the defence was Dr Gloster's accredited expertise in midwifery and the unlikely attribution of such a bungled 'operation' to one of his considerable experience. There was something peculiar about Eliza's anatomy however, which quite possibly contributed to error on the part of whoever undertook her examination on that fateful occasion and 'passed an instrument' in the process - her uterus lay at an unusual angle, such that a medical practitioner unfamiliar with her reproductive physique might easily misinterpret physical resistance offered to the intrusion of an otherwise innocuous probe.

These very details are owing to none other than Dr Thomas Bond, who, on cross examination in his capacity as an expert witness, made the following observations:

> I have performed several post mortem examinations on women on whom abortion had been performed – I should expect an unskilled man to make such a wound more than a skilled man.

> I have never seen such a wound caused by the act of a skilled man. I do not think it would be accidental.

> I heard Dr Gloster's qualifications read here today. I should say they were good. I think more than ordinarily good.

On re-examination however, he revealed the not insignificant structural detail regarding the patient's uterus:

> I don't think it would require much skill to pass the cotton wool to the part where the wound had already reached –

> My reason for that is that the womb I think was bent a little at the internal os and instead of going straight into the cavity the instrument would naturally impinge on the wall of the same place.

Of course mistakes can, and do, happen. As for Dr Gloster's qualifications being 'more than ordinarily good', whilst Dr Crane concurred in that regard, Dr Frankish held a contrary opinion.

> Dr Crane:

> I saw Dr Gloster's qualifications in the Medical Directory. They are good – above the average.

> Dr Frankish:

> I don't think defendant's qualifications above the average – they are average qualifications. – I don't know the name of the obstetric certificate. I don't think the Dublin qualification equal to the English.

A few background checks would appear to be in order. Hence it is appropriate we consider the personal history of the esteemed (at least by himself) Doctor James Gloster; a history which entails rather more than a cursory glance at the Medical Directory might suggest.

Born into a landowning family of some local significance, James Cockburn Gloster, native of Rockfield, Limerick, would go on to fulfil a professional destiny in adulthood such as might be expected of any Victorian gentleman. The army, the church, medicine or law being the conventional assembly points, James Gloster opted for, or was otherwise deposited in, medicine, an arena requiring both aptitude and intellect. Whilst he may have been in earnest possession of the latter, he could not be said to have been instinctively drawn to the profession of his (or just as likely others') choosing. Consequently his progress in the field was somewhat less than meteoric.

According to the Medical Directory for 1888 at least, Dr Gloster was a graduate of Dublin (MB, MCh) and a Licentiate in Midwifery from the Rotunda Hospital there. His professional credentials included that of (late) House Surgeon at the St Marylebone General Dispensary, then at 77 Welbeck St., W1. James Gloster was in fact Resident Medical Officer for the Dispensary from May 1883 until May the following year, when he was obliged to resign after it became known that he had set up in private practice without prior reference to his current employers.

No less significant is the Medical Directory's reference to Gloster as (late) House Physician at the London Hospital, Whitechapel, where he had previously (1882) attended for 'surgical practice' as a student on six months special admission.

There is no evidence that Dr James Gloster ever held a post-graduate position of any kind at the London Hospital. He does not appear in the hospital's own register of House Surgeons and Physicians. His claim via the Medical Directory was therefore spurious, predicated upon nothing more, it would seem, than a fleeting and largely unsuccessful period of studentship several years previously. (His record of attendance covers barely half the intended six-month period, whilst Surgeon Mr Warren Tay's comment on his performance as a 'Dresser' is on record as 'very poor'. Not exactly the stuff of which professional eminence is made.)

The private practice in which Dr Gloster set himself up while still in the employ of the St Marylebone Dispensary was, of course, that which he administered from 15 Upper Phillimore Place, West Kensington; a decidedly 'up-market' address, which has since been assimilated into Kensington High Street. Moreton Place Pimlico is some distance away, but walking between the two locales is at least feasible, provided one has the time to spare.

The near neighbour who 'sometimes assisted' at Dr Gloster's Phillimore Road practice was one Meredith Townsend, a Kensington resident of some standing. Abiding at 24 Phillimore Place, this gentleman was a member of the Royal College of Surgeons, England, Licentiate of the Society of Apothecaries (1868), and Medical Officer for the Central District, Kensington.

We know, because he has stated as much, that Dr Louis Tarrico, accoucheur, of 22 Wardour Street, was personally acquainted with Dr James Gloster, who for the past few years had 'sent him customers'. Whereas a connection between a male midwife based in Soho and another in Kensington might not appear too outlandish, given that they once worked in the same geographical area for a time, Dr Townsend's familiarity with Tarrico's practice (if it were Townsend who pre-emptively referred Eliza Schummacher - her oral statement is a touch ambiguous in that regard) would be rather more difficult to explain.

Dr Gloster's later life would not be without personal tragedy. His only son, Henry Colpoys Gloster, sadly died during the First World War. Barely twenty years of age, he was serving as a lieutenant with the 6th battalion, the Gordon Highlanders, when, in March 1915, he was killed while occupying a German trench with his platoon during the battle of Neuve Chapelle.

Curiously however, and of rather more interest in the present context, young Henry's obituary, as published in the services Roll of Honour, describes him as the only son of Dr James Cockburn Gloster B.A., MB. The abbreviated reference to a qualification in surgery is missing.

CHAPTER 5

A HINT OF JUNIPER

Taken at face value, Eliza Schummacher's dying statement makes the cause of her fatal misfortune perfectly clear – a botched operation. But was she being wholly honest? Did the events, as she described them, fall into line with her sister's account, for instance? It is said that 'Hell hath no fury like a woman scorned'. Might her indignation at being spurned in her hour of need have perhaps driven Eliza to implicate Dr James Gloster, purely out of spite, as he himself suggested? No woman appreciates being 'stood up' after all, even by a doctor, and Eliza was understandably angry when she sent for him. She was after all his friend as well as his patient, according to Dr Louis Tarrico.

Furthermore, at the time Dr Crane transcribed the poor woman's testimony, there was nothing in the way of evidence to suggest the immediate cause of her impending death. More obvious grounds for suspicion were offered by the 'medicine' her sister Emily had dutifully administered previously. Most of the 8 oz. bottle had been consumed by the late afternoon of Friday the 27th June, and stomach pains, as everyone knows, can easily result from poisoning of some kind.

The mysterious little bottle did indeed contain a toxin. With a 'nose' for pharmaceuticals to rival that of a wine fancier, Dr Crane adjudged it to have contained, not a compound of rhubarb, but tincture of Ergot of Rye - an abortifacient.

Like the bony digit of a beached skeleton on Treasure Island therefore, that observation alone pointed to Eliza's accusations' incorporating an element of truth at the very least. It was not the only potion to have passed Eliza's lips during those few days however, as sister Emily later revealed:

> On Monday or Tuesday when she was ill I did give her a little spirits; not on both days, but on the Tuesday. It was in my sister's house. I got it on the Monday evening myself. I can't say if I sent Mrs Burles on Wednesday. I think my sister sent her away. I complained to my sister of Mrs Burles taking the spirits. I said there was more taken of the spirits than there should have been and my sister couldn't have taken it. I made the complaint on Tuesday, when I came in from dinner that more spirits had been taken than ought to have been. I asked if she had taken any - she said no. That was between 3 and 3.30 p.m. on Tuesday.
>
> I didn't speak to Mrs Burles about it that afternoon. The spirits were kept on the ground floor at times. On the Tuesday morning before I went to dinner I took them upstairs to 2nd floor back room to mix my sister some gin and water. The front room on that floor is a workroom – the back where we take our meals. When I mixed the spirits I found Mrs Burles downstairs.

One of Emily Maud's early preoccupations, it would seem, was the spirit level visible within the Gin bottle! Just how much should have been consumed by her 'sober' sister, one wonders, before she (Emily) would suspect Mrs Burles of having sampled it? In-house worker Mrs Burles, on the other hand, denied all knowledge of any spirits. "I never saw any spirits in the house at any time", she reported straightforwardly.

At this stage in our story the small matter of who had access to the Gin, and how often, may appear something of a digression. It is however a consideration which would assume greater importance as the investigation into the death of Eliza Schummacher progressed.

*

The police in late Victorian London were heavily dependent on 'leg-work'; that, horse-drawn transport and the telegraph system. They were nevertheless diligent despite the difficulties, and the rigor of their investigation would gradually reveal itself in this case. Eliza Schummacher's dying statement may have set them on a pre-determined path, but one thing they cannot be accused of is not following up all the relevant leads.

Going by appearances, and placing due legal weight upon the dying declaration of the deceased, the police proceeded to arrest the two men she had explicitly identified: doctors Louis Tarrico and James Gloster, each of whom expressed both surprise at the accusation and differing degrees of ignorance with regard to the relevant events. The inquest that ensued would highlight the gravity of the charges to follow.

The early depositions of inspector Burner, sergeants Manley and Clough explain the situation perfectly clearly.

> Edward Burner, Inspector, B division, on oath says:
>
> At ten minutes past three yesterday afternoon, in company with Sergeant Manley, I went to 15 Upper Phillimore Place Kensington. I there saw Dr Gloster. He lived there. I said, "We are Police Officers and have come upon a rather serious matter. You must consider yourself in custody on suspicion of causing the death of Eliza Schummacher." He said, "I know nothing

about it." I said to him, "Doctor, whatever you say will be repeated in evidence, therefore I must caution you." He said, "Her sister came to me and said that her sister was in a certain way. I sent her to another Doctor and he attended her." I asked him for his visiting book which he gave me. He said, "You will find no entry in there and as I did not attend her I made no entry. I have not made up my book but there are my lists." He gave me several lists of people he called on. I said to him the statement that had been taken by Dr Crane. He said, "I don't know what made her say that when she was dying - it must be spite, you don't know her - she is a bad drunken woman." I then took him to Gerald Road Police Station where he was detained. About 3 o'clock this morning he was charged with Dr Tarrico. He made no reply to the charge.

About 12 o'clock last night I was present with Sergeants Manley, Clough and Bowden when Dr Tarrico was arrested at 22 Wardour St., Soho. He spoke very imperfect English and Sergeant Clough carried on the conversation in Italian with him.

Thomas Manley, Sergeant, B division, on oath says:

Last night about 12 o'clock, I went in company with Inspector Burner and Sergeants Clough and Bowden to 22 Wardour Street, Soho, where I saw prisoner Tarrico. I told him I was a Police Officer and should take him into custody for being concerned with Dr Gloster on suspicion of causing the death of Eliza Schummacher (She died on Wednesday night last about 12 o'clock at 21 Moreton Place, Pimlico). He said, "I do not understand what you say." The charge was then explained to him in Italian by Sergeant Clough. We went upstairs. I searched his rooms and took possession of a quantity of surgical instruments. I then conveyed him to Gerald Road Police Station, where he was charged with Dr Gloster. He made no reply in answer to the charge when it was read over to him.

Edward Clough, Sergeant, B division, on oath says:

At 12 o'clock last night I accompanied Inspector Burner, Sergeant Manley and Sergeant Bowden to 22 Wardour Street, Soho, where I saw Dr Tarrico at the door. I explained to him what we had come for. He quite understood me. He replied "I know nothing about it." I went upstairs with the Inspector and the other Sergeants and cautioned him as to what he said.

Two doctors, both arrested on suspicion. But suspicion of what exactly? Neither Dr Gloster's visiting book nor his lists of pending entries made any mention of a patient by the name of Eliza Schummacher. Yet before passing away she made sure Dr Crane and others understood that Tarrico and Gloster had each 'passed an instrument'. Whereas the former had been 'gentle', the latter, she asserted, was responsible for 'tearing her insides to pieces', as well as supplying the ergot afterwards.

That Eliza Schummacher did not die as a result of imbibing a toxic cocktail of some kind may be gathered from other witness accounts. The Gin, it has to be said, relates more to motive than method. Eliza's sister Emily, having recounted her own fleeting suspicions concerning the alcohol, also had something to say about blood:

> On 18th June I noticed marks on my sister's chemise. She was in bed. I saw blood about 6.30 p.m. It was fresh blood - quite wet. She continued to wear it till the Sunday following. I put her on a clean one on Sunday, clean clothes and clean bedding. I noticed a little show of blood continuously every day on her chemise. There was still a slight show till her death. I didn't notice there was blood on the sheets. Before I changed the sheets on Sunday there were. The chemises and sheets have been washed since.

The definitive determination, however, was made by Dr Thomas Bond, who conducted the autopsy. Dr Crane was present to assist and to verify, Dr Frankish also. (Surgeon to the police at Westminster, Dr Bond would go on to play an equally significant role in further murderous events later that autumn.)

Those of a squeamish disposition might prefer at this point to take it as read that Eliza Schummacher was violated internally, and that this intrusion led to her death. Dr Bond's findings were distressing, and remain so. The following is his account given before the magistrate, Mr d'Eyncourt. (His report before the Coroner was considerably more gruesome!)

Thomas Bond. Sworn:

I live at 7 the Sanctuary. I am a Fellow of the Royal College of Surgeons. I am a surgeon at Westminster Hospital and was a lecturer for several years on Forensic Medicine.

I saw the body of Mrs Schummacher at the mortuary on the 30th June – I then made a post mortem examination, doctors Crane and Frankish being present – I believe at the request of the Coroner.

I made the post mortem personally. I found no injury until I got to the uterus. When I proceeded to open the uterus I found a wound in the posterior wall of the uterus passing directly upwards in the posterior wall until it emerged on the peritoneal surface of the pelvic cavity. The point of emergence was near the top of the uterus. It was rather to the left-hand side. I made a mistake before the Coroner in saying the right-hand side. It was more towards the left hand side of the woman.

The depth from the beginning of the hole until it emerged on the peritoneal surface was about two inches. I found where the hole in the walls of the uterus emerged into the peritoneal cavity the hole was glued up with lymph. Before I had made this examination of the uterus I had found a piece of cotton wool lying near the upper part of the uterus. When I took it out it was about 2 inches in length as it lay down without being pressed, and saturated with lymph it looked about the size of a tube I hold, from ¾ to ½ an inch in diameter. I am certain that wound must have been inflicted during life. I think the wound might have been caused by an uterine sound or any instrument similar to an uterine sound. Considerable force must have been used. The cotton wool might have been carried in with the instrument that inflicted the injury. Certainly if carried in with the instrument more force must have been used than that for the passage of the instrument without the wool.

I think the instrument might possibly have been withdrawn and then repassed with the cotton wool to the same place. It is possible. I don't see any improbability in it – I think, the infliction of the wound would cause blood to flow. The infliction of such a wound must have caused great pain either with wool or without. Supposing the wool was carried in with the second insertion of the instrument that would cause pain – after the infliction of that wound the woman could not have walked about and carried on her usual society – not for long – I shouldn't think she could walk about after 24 hours. I think inflammation would have started causing great pain, I think great pain would have been caused from the time of the infliction of the injury. I formed no opinion as to the length of time the wound had been inflicted in consequence of finding organised lymph adherent to the peritoneal surface of the uterus and from the advanced stage of peritonitis in which I found the pelvic cavity and the intestinal peritoneum.

I thought it must have been done at least a week before death – it may have been longer – I hardly think three weeks but I think it may have been more than a fortnight – I cannot fix it any nearer than that.

The effect of such a wound would be to cause peritonitis which would get worse and worse.

Peritonitis was the cause of death. The probable effect of such wound would be to lay the woman up at once. – I have not had personal experience of such wounds. I merely judge from general knowledge.

I have no doubt that the cause of death was peritonitis caused by the wound and the wool in the place I found it.

That wound could not have been effected by the careless use of the syringe produced. I can't answer the question as to the wound being inflicted by a person having a slight knowledge of anatomy.

A competent man could not have inflicted such a wound without gross carelessness.

I found no evidence of disease among the other organs beyond slight adhesions at the apex of the lungs. It is quite clear she was not pregnant. There was no sign of any tumour.

CHAPTER 6

MEN AND MONEY

Within the framework of the Victorian age one might easily be tempted to view Eliza Jane Schummacher with a disproportionate degree of sympathy. Not yet enfranchised, the women of Victorian England were, from top to toe, subordinate components of the social system. Be that as it may, the female of the species, individually even if not collectively, was as determined a character as ever, albeit obliged to operate under a considerable degree of constraint. From 'Vicky dearest' at the top to 'Pearly Poll' at the bottom, ladies of whatever class had ways and means of getting their own way, or simply surviving, paying the rent or scraping together their 'doss money'. It was ever thus, and Eliza Jane was no exception. She was a woman first, a victim second.

If that all sounds dreadfully misogynistic, it is important to keep a close watch on the practicalities of Mrs Schummacher's situation, and not allow the clichéd 'veneer' of Victorian comportment to obscure the realities of her adult life. Her sister, Emily Maud Baker, who visited regularly to assist with work at Moreton Place, was understandably ready to attest to Eliza's good character, as upstanding, industrious, and by no means a drunkard. As she deposed (on the 17th July):

> She was far from a drunken woman. She was highly respected, worked at her milliner's business and was a sober woman.

A view endorsed by another sister, Agnes Beresford, who the following month (the 14th August) testified:

> I used to see my sister every fortnight or three
> weeks – she was certainly not a drunken woman.

As forewarned, however, witness statements from all quarters in this case leave much to be desired as regards consistency. Emily Maud's are no exception, as we shall see in due course, but a line of reasoning follows immediately and inevitably from this one unsolicited character reference, 'solicitation' being the operative word. It was a line subtly pursued in Dr Gloster's defence.

Mrs Schummacher was described (and described herself) as a 'dress and mantle maker'. She did not make hats. That would be the job of a milliner. Hence it is somewhat curious that Emily Maud Baker, who more than occasionally had a hand in the business, should refer to it as 'millinery'. One might also bear in mind that many a lady engaged in the 'oldest profession' in Victorian London adopted the title 'sempstress' with which to mask their more clandestine activities.

Again, according to her sister Emily, Mrs Schummacher was out 'on business' daily ("For the purposes of the business it was necessary for her to go out every day to see customers", she said when recalled to the witness stand on the 24th July), whilst two flights upstairs at Moreton Place she had several female lodgers.

Now keeping a lodger or two is not that unusual a practice among those occupying large houses, but, as Emily Maud once again informs us, *these* ladies were not necessarily up and about *their* business elsewhere during the day as one might ordinarily expect. Speaking of events on the Tuesday, Emily explains, under cross-examination, how:

> One of the workers of my sister generally
> opened the door. I have when I have been
> there. There was no servant in the house.

There was my sister, Mrs Burles and Miss
Barnes in the house. I have made a mistake.
Miss Barnes was not there on the Tuesday.
There were lodgers in the house – women
lodgers. I went up on the second floor. I heard
the street door shut that's all.

'There were women lodgers', plural, in the house during the day,
one of them identified by another witness (needleworker, Mary
Hull) as a Mrs Ambler:

I have lived at 21 Moreton Place. I remember
deceased dying on Wednesday. On Monday
week (the 18th) before she died I recollect her
coming down into the kitchen. I believe it was
about 2.30 to 3. It was after 2. I really couldn't
say what time it was. She came down for a jug
of hot water. Mrs Ambler, a lodger, was in the
room. She asked for a jug of water, took it and
went upstairs. I went into the front kitchen, my
room, and sat there doing needlework.

Mary Hull clearly distinguishes between herself as an employee
and Mrs Ambler, 'a lodger'. So what were the lodgers doing all the
while they were at the house?

That seems to have been a question which crossed the mind of
Gloster's advocate, Mr Gill, even if it did not cross his lips in open
court. Others of a similar vein no doubt did, as both Emily Maud
and in-house worker Mrs Burles were obliged, for the record, to
discuss certain personal details that might be viewed as having
rather more to do with the employer's lifestyle than an unskilled
medic's physical intrusion into her person.

Emily Maud Baker:

> I worked in the business with my sister. She had
> not spoken to me about being pregnant not till
> about 2 or 3 months ago. She had two children
> by her marriage.
>
> She told me 2 or 3 months before her death she
> thought she was in the family way. I do not
> know of her having had miscarriages during the
> last 4 or 5 years. I don't say my sister told me all
> her private affairs – she didn't tell me about her
> private affairs.

Mrs Burles:

> I was not there in the evenings – I don't know
> where she went then. On Monday I saw her
> when she came up. I don't know when she
> came in. I didn't see her till she had her things
> off. It was on the Monday afternoon she told
> me she had been to Kensington, to a Lady
> Somebody – I can't remember. I was up and
> down, in and out, of Mrs Schummacher's room
> on the Tuesday. I might have had my hand on
> the door when Dr Gloster came out. It was not
> fastened in any way.

Other features which might colour one's interpretation of the
goings on at 21 Moreton Place, Pimlico, include the geography of the
accommodation, with Eliza Schummacher sleeping downstairs (in the
hospitality suite?), and a certain transience on the part of visitors to
the property; something clearly alluded to by counsel. Mary Hull
divulged further (redacted) detail under cross examination:

The kitchen is below the level of the street, the window looks out on an area surrounded by walls. The area is one and a half yards wide I believe. It may be more. There is no table in front of the window. The area is not covered with a grating. There are iron railings to the area. I was sitting sideways looking toward the street door. I turned quite round when I heard the door go. I had been facing the door when I heard it. I turned quite round I can't see the front door. Victoria Station was at my back. There is a door step and one step to the railings.

Men would take 5 or 6 steps I think to get past the window.

Semantically, there is a real and very relevant difference between a generalised singular instance (e.g., 'a man might take', or 'would take') and the more specific plural form. The statement, 'Men would take 5 or 6 steps' tells us quite plainly that 'men' did so. Furthermore, and given these events took place in Victorian London, how many men of the period might one expect to visit a dressmaker's atelier in connection with a dress?

The 16th August statement of Louise Ambler herself raises as many questions as it affords answers:

> I live with my mother and father at 41 Moreton Place. (What was she doing at no. 21 therefore?) I knew the deceased. I recollect her dying.
>
> The day (actually the week) before she died, on a Tuesday the 19th, I remember drawing some water on the landing between the dining and drawing room floor. It was some

time I think between 1 and 3. I heard the handle
of the back dining room (the deceased's
bedroom) turn. I looked down and I saw a
gentleman come out of her bedroom door. I
didn't stop to see which room he went. He went
into the front room. I heard his steps. I went to
the first floor bedroom with the water. I thought
I heard someone talking rather loud, a woman's
voice. I couldn't recognize defendant in the
gentleman I saw. I recollect the first day I came
to the Police Court I was shown between 16 and
20 men. I saw the defendant and I picked him
out as the gentleman I had seen on the 19th.

Further to which Mr Gill, cross examining, probably felt he had
tapped a promising seam himself, given a witness who could not
recognize his client as the man she saw leave Eliza Schummacher's
Moreton Place bedroom, yet afterwards goes on to 'pick him out'
- *as the man she had seen.*

I had not seen men come to the house in the
evening. I didn't know if any man came there or
not – I think there was one man friend visited
Mrs Schummacher. I saw him once, not during
the illness – before that, a long time.

Again, as with Mary Hull, we have reference to 'men' coming
and going. 'Frailty, thy name is woman.' And among a woman's
frailties are, predictably, members of the opposite sex.

*

On the grounds that a machine worker is rather more likely to
maintain a straight line when sober, it is reasonably safe to assume
that at number 21 the hallowed gin bottle was kept in the house

for entertainment purposes, not shared among the troops so as to encourage performance. This was Pimlico, not Prussia, but gin was still a useful asset, as Emily Maud informed the court:

> I complained to my sister of Mrs Burles taking
> the spirits. I said there was more taken of the
> spirits than there should have and my sister
> couldn't have taken it.

It is undeniably the case however that Eliza Schummacher was the better placed to help herself to a tot or two should she have wished. Mrs Burles worked upstairs, while the gin was lodged downstairs, according to Emily Maud:

> The spirits were kept on the ground floor at times.

'At times'. When entertaining, no doubt. Acknowledging the specific gravity of the issue, Mrs Burles would have none of it, as she herself claimed:

> I never saw any spirits in the house that day.

And there is further curious evidence concerning yet another female to consider. Once more it emerges through a statement of Emily Maud's:

> When I mixed the spirits I found Mrs Burles
> downstairs. My sister mostly wrote her own letters.
> Sometimes other persons wrote for her. I decline
> to give any name. It was a female person. I decline
> to give the name – a person named Mrs Fanny
> Gardener – I don't know her address.

She declines to give a name, but gives it anyway. She continues:

> But she has not been with my sister for over
> two years.

43

I saw her last at my sister's house, or at her apartments. She is a dress maker. The last time I knew her she was living with my sister at 24 Moreton Place. I saw her there about two years ago – not since. My sister has been in Moreton place seven years at different addresses. I don't know where Gardener is now. I don't know where she works. She worked with my sister and has worked for my sister for years. She has no father. I don't know if she has a mother. I know nothing about her, only what I have seen of her at work. I dare say it's quite two years ago I last saw her.

My sister could read and write. I did not see letters from Gardener to my sister. My sister generally burnt the letters as she received them. She had no letters at her death only one, two. My eldest sister has them (margin note: on reading over she says 'after her death').

I objected to give the name of Gardener because I didn't think she had anything to do with this case. I don't know that my sister had any one to conduct her correspondence during the last two or three months.

So (the possibly orphaned) Fanny Gardener, *another* dress maker, lodged for an unspecified period of time at Moreton Place with Eliza Schummacher, and Emily Maud, for reasons best known to herself, arbitrarily concluded she was irrelevant to the case! Was it the nature of Fanny Gardener's earlier career which Emily would rather not have introduced, the possibility that her sister Eliza was not altogether the literate professional she was portrayed as being, or both?

Fanny Gardener's name came up in connection with correspondence, not simply *with* Eliza Schummacher but written on her behalf. "My sister could read and write", said Emily defensively. Others were less certain. Mrs Burles deposed:

> She said then (On Tuesday) "I wish *you* could
> go and send a telegram." She gave the name
> 'Dr Gloster, High Street Kensington'.

> 'Come to Norton Place at once'.

> I sent the telegram and wrote it. She dictated
> it. *She could not write.*

Eliza's understandable incapacity extended primarily to her legs, not her arms, while Fanny's sister, Georgina Gardener, had most definitely acted as scribe for Eliza once or twice:

> I live at 1 Hanover Rd. Pimlico, am a dress maker.

> (Just how many 'dress makers' could the
> Pimlico district have supported?)

> I knew deceased Mrs Schummacher. I worked
> for her one day about six weeks before she died
> and about a few weeks two years ago. I then wrote
> one or two business letters for her. None besides.

> I have not written one since.

Fanny Garwood (née Gardener) herself conducted business correspondence for Mrs Schummacher, the last time two years previously, but what she says under cross-examination, of yet another Gardener sister (Eugenie), is no less intriguing:

> Years ago she knew Mrs Schummacher, not recently as she didn't care for Mrs Schummacher.

Of course we do not know exactly how good a general judge of character Eugenie Gardener was, but there is little doubting the direction that Mr Gill's questions were inviting the court to take in its assessment of the deceased Eliza Schummacher. From Emily Maud's reference to her sister's two children by marriage, coupled with ignorance of her several possible miscarriages, we may understand Mrs Schummacher to have been perfectly well aware that to skate on thin ice is to risk an accident - a risk she was quite prepared to take it would seem. She must have believed, after all, that she had good grounds for announcing her unwanted pregnancy to Emily Maud *before* it was clinically confirmed (as indeed it never was).

Little by little, Gill teased out from the various witnesses the names of several men, who, one way or another, were considered to be of some relevance to the matter of Eliza Schummacher's death through malpractice. One at least was known to have visited her at 21 Moreton Place. For others it was largely a question of suspicion.

Whether personal or professional, Eliza Schummacher's dalliances cannot alter the fact that she was undoubtedly the victim of a criminal assault, of which someone, most probably a man, was guilty. Mr Gill, however, was not seeking to exonerate his client simply on account of questionable behaviour on the part of the deceased, but drawing attention, albeit indirectly, to the reliability of her accusation, and her motive for bringing it in the direction she did. A lady of impeccable character might not be expected to lie about such things. A lady of dubious character on the other hand...

A good legal advocate never came cheap. The affluent Dr Gloster had in Mr Gill a fellow countryman skilled enough to see him later involved in the notorious 'Baccarat Trial' of 1891 and the subsequent prosecution of Oscar Wilde. He served as Recorder of Chichester for more than thirty years (1890 – 1921). Bizarrely, even Eliza Schummacher was posthumously credited by the prosecution with some of Gloster's money, in the form of a cheque, which she claimed to have been invited to cash on the doctor's behalf.

*

The 'tale of the token' centres on a visit to Dr Gloster's practice, which Eliza Schummacher claimed to have made (on the 4th June ostensibly). Her sister Emily Maud, who "never saw Dr Gloster ('at my sister's house')", commented upon a piece of paper produced in court and "said by my sister to be in Dr Gloster's handwriting. It is a request to change a cheque."

Under cross examination she was more forthcoming:

> She gave me the paper 3 (i.e., Exhibit 3) on Friday before she died in the presence of Dr Crane. She was in bed at the time.
>
> I took it off her dressing table. That was the first I had seen it.
>
> She said I have a piece of paper Dr Gloster gave to me on the Monday I went to him. He gave me £5 cheque to change opposite to his house. It was folded and had been placed under a little desk on the dressing table.
>
> It was folded in 4 with the corner bent down.
>
> She didn't mention the date when she got this. I think she said on the Monday, I am not quite sure – she got it in the morning. I think she said on the Monday. I looked on the date when I

> gave it to Dr Crane. I have not looked to see
> what day it was – I think she said she got it in
> the morning.

Despite a certain ambiguity concerning the location of the dressing table in this account, it is nevertheless clear that Eliza Schummacher revealed to her sister, not just a slip of paper in Dr Gloster's handwriting, but that he had entrusted to Eliza a cheque for £5 (a tidy sum) to be cashed by her across the road. There was, however, no clarification as to what became of the money, nor why it came Eliza's way, if indeed it ever did so, although she appeared to be in possession of a docket of sorts.

This episode is very much a double-edged sword. On the one hand it lends weight to Eliza's account of a visit to Doctor Gloster's surgery, of which he claimed to have kept no record. Conversely, it might be construed as suggesting that, rather than the doctor receiving a guinea for his consultation, he was actually in the process of paying the patient; but for what?

The defendant, Doctor Gloster, offered his own explanation for the slip of paper latterly in Mrs Schummacher's possession. Unsurprisingly it did not dovetail with that of prosecution witness Emily Maud:

> I did not (on this occasion) ask her to change a
> cheque for me at Mr Buckle's.

> The piece of paper which has been produced
> was written for the purpose of being taken over
> by one of my servants and Mrs Schummacher
> must have picked it up in the room while
> waiting for me.

Recalled and re-examined, Emily Maud ratified, albeit circuitously, the defendant's timing of this event:

I don't know that I mentioned any date when
my sister said she had been to Gloster. She said
she had been to Dr Gloster when she saw the
assistant, she went a second time when Dr
Gloster gave her the cheque – that was after she
had seen the assistant, the piece of paper was
the proof she said so. Dr Crane asked her the
date. She said she couldn't say, but the date was
on the paper.

11th June it is then, and Eliza Schummacher returns home from
nearby Kensington High Street with a piece of paper and,
presumably, the proceeds of a transaction at a local post office.
But then Eliza's own version of events rocks the boat:

> *He came to see me here on the 11th June* and
> he again passed an instrument which hurt me
> very much.

Where is the evidence that Gloster visited Eliza Schummacher
at 21 Moreton Place either earlier in the day on the 11th June
(before she called upon *him* and picked up the piece of paper) or
afterwards? And what did Mr Buckle's employee, Samuel Spark,
have to say about the cashing of cheques? Precisely this:

> I am cashier to Mr Buckle. He lives at 1
> Newland Terrace Kensington.
>
> He keeps the post office there as a grocer.
>
> I know defendant by sight. He lives nearly
> opposite the Post Office – I have cashed
> cheques for Dr Gloster. I do not know that I
> have cashed for strangers from Dr Gloster.

I have not had notes with his cheques that I am
aware of.

Cheque produced 11th June £5. I can't say if I
cashed it for Dr Gloster.

On 11th June I cashed five cheques. I can't say if
this was one. I enter them. My employer's
Bank is the London & County Kensington, a
stamp of the bank not ours. I can't remember if
paper B was shown to me on 9th June. It might
have accompanied a cheque of that date.

Cross examined the witness said:

If paper B was brought by a stranger I should
have kept it. I know one of Dr Gloster's servants
by sight. She has come to cash cheques.

Re-examined he said:

I ought not to have cashed the cheque without
keeping the paper.

He then added:

It is not probable that the paper could have
been shown me with the cheque without my
retaining the paper.

On the basis that a cheque is its own receipt, Samuel Sparks
was prepared to cash cheques in favour of Mr Buckle's near
neighbour, Dr Gloster, provided they were brought in by a
member of his staff, whom Sparks would recognize. Under such
circumstances *they were not usually accompanied by written
instruction.* Otherwise (and probably in his own defence), Sparks
said he should have kept the chitty as a counterfoil.

But what did Dr Gloster say, again?

> The piece of paper which has been produced
> was written *for the purpose of being taken over
> by one of my servants* and Mrs Schummacher
> must have picked it up in the room while
> waiting for me.

It appears *this* instruction to 'pay the bearer' was written for a
purpose not usually observed. Might it therefore have been written
for Eliza Schummacher's benefit after all?

CHAPTER 7

VISITING HOURS

We know well what befell Mrs Eliza Schummacher. What is less certain is when. A convincing answer to that question might go a long way toward determining the identity of the party ultimately responsible for her death. At autopsy Dr Bond fixed, as nearly as he was able, the date when the fatal wound could have been administered:

> I thought it must have been done at least a week
> before death – it may have been longer – I
> hardly think three weeks, but I think it may have
> been more than a fortnight – I cannot fix it any
> nearer than that.

The comings and goings of Eliza, her sister and others around this time are of some importance therefore. Here, in his own words, is another of Dr Bond's significant findings:

> After the infliction of that wound the woman
> could not have walked about and carried on her
> usual society – not for long – I shouldn't think
> she could walk about after 24 hours.

These are the very real clinical constraints which must apply to the witnesses' varying accounts of what transpired during the month of June 1888.

Understandably devoid of certain detail, Eliza Schummacher's own (redacted) declaration incorporated the following essentials:

She went to see Dr Gloster at 15 Upper Phillimore Place, who said he could not have anything to do with her. She had mentioned it to a gentleman at Dr Gloster's who sometimes assisted him. He said go to Dr Tarrico. He told her to ask Dr Tarrico if he would examine her and if Dr Tarrico did so examine her then he, Dr Gloster, would take on the case.

She then went, on the same day, to Dr Tarrico, and he gently passed an instrument. ('That was last Thursday four weeks'). Next day Dr Gloster passed an instrument which hurt very much. He visited 21 Moreton Place on the 11th June and again very painfully passed an instrument. Afterwards in agony and unable to get up, Eliza sent for Dr Gloster. He did not pass an instrument that day but brought some medicine and applied some cotton wool, saying it would stop the pain. She thought he had left the cotton wool inside her and did not see him again.

Two things are evident here. First, it is not at all clear, from Eliza's statement, which party referred her to Dr Tarrico. Second, the 48-hour period prior to the 11th June, when she acted upon this referral and afterwards paid a follow-up visit to Dr Gloster, is not exactly specified in time. Hence we must turn to the depositions of others in order to re-construct more precisely the possible sequence of events as they unfolded. Dealing with them in chronological order, we might look to Eliza's sister Emily Maud Baker to fill the first gaps in the account.

Emily Maud's version of their trip to Soho has herself and Eliza (who complained only of a pain in her back) visiting Dr Tarrico in Wardour Street, then Stag and Mantles at Leicester Square, on the 8th June. On parting company Eliza walked home normally:

> On Friday 8th June I went to her house by appointment. I went with her after shopping to 22 Wardour Street. I didn't know that address before (although Eliza must have done). It was about 3.30 p.m. when we left. We went to Stagg

and Mantles and from there travelled together
to her house, 21 Moreton Place. I next saw my
sister on the Saturday week after (the 16ᵗʰ). I saw
her at her own house. She had sent for me – *she
was up and dressed and doing her work in the
ordinary way. She then appeared to be in her
usual health.*

It looks then as if Eliza Schummacher was already familiar with
Dr Tarrico's location before arriving there in her sister's company.
Eight days later she is out of bed, and active. Two days more and
she's bed-ridden. Might the fatal wound(s) have been administered
that weekend therefore? (Emily Maud did not stay beyond 11.00
a.m. on the Saturday, nor did she arrive on the Monday until after
4.00 p.m.) Oddly, Emily contradicts an unimportant detail under
cross-examination:

> When we went to Stagg and Mantles, she told
> me she was going to Wardour Street.

(Meaning, '*we* were going to Wardour Street', which they had
presumably yet to visit, and not straight home after all.) She also repeats
Eliza's references to her commerce with Dr Gloster; an account that
includes a further, and rather more consequential, contradiction:

> When she was ill I questioned my sister who she
> had had and she told me – I think that was on
> the Wednesday morning or Tuesday evening.
> *My sister did not tell me* that she had been to *Dr
> Gloster* to do something for her as she was in the
> family way and he *would have nothing to do with
> her.* She didn't use those words.
>
> She said she had been to Dr Gloster at his
> house. *She didn't say that he at his house had*

54

told her he would have nothing to do with her.
She said she had gone to Dr Gloster to do
something for her.

Dr Gloster had attended a child of hers 2 or 3
years before – she had not seen him for 2 or 3 years,
not to my knowledge (note: to *her* knowledge), - she
said she had been to Dr Gloster and he was out.
She saw the other gentleman that assisted him. She
told him what she wanted; her business that had
called her there. The assistant said he was sure Dr
Gloster would not do it for her. She waited for Dr
Gloster and saw him. She didn't mention that the
assistant had told her to go away – *my sister said that
Dr Gloster said when he heard what she wanted he
couldn't have anything to do with her* but she must
go to Dr Tarrico. She told me she had gone to Dr
Tarrico on the Monday (4th) before the Friday 8th
June. She did not tell me the time of the day she
had seen him nor who was present nor in what
room it was. She never said, that I know of, that she
had ever been to Dr Gloster's house, except on that
one occasion.

'That one occasion', Monday the 4th June, was also the day Dr
Gloster is said by her sister Emily to have passed Eliza the £5
cheque, following which she took herself off to Dr Tarrico, or so
she maintained. But, as 'Exhibit 3' amply confirms, Dr Gloster's
'memo' in that regard, as well as the postmarked envelope on
which it was written, each bear the date of the intended transaction
- 11th June. The request addressed to Mr Buckle was most
probably prepared either later that morning or early that
afternoon, as whatever the envelope originally contained it must

first have been delivered to Dr Gloster's home address before *he* could have written on it.

What then of Eliza's own claim that 'next day Dr Gloster passed an instrument which hurt very much'? As Emily Maud made clear, Eliza was not given to revealing every detail of her private life. Tarrico himself deposed how he first encountered Eliza Schummacher (presumably) about 8 or 10 days prior to his own arrest (at midnight on Sunday the 1st July). She was accompanied by Dr Gloster, who introduced her personally and left with her afterwards.

Unless Tarrico's estimate is wildly inaccurate therefore, his first meeting with the importunate Eliza Schummacher took place much nearer the 18th June than either the 4th or the 11th, and by that same evening she was bed-ridden. Perhaps we should appeal to the co-accused for clarification:

> I recollect attending a child of the deceased woman between 3 and 4 years ago. I did not see her again until the evening of *the fifth of June* last when, on going home late, my friend and neighbour Dr Townsend, who had been called in by one of my servants, told me a patient was in the dining room and had said she was in the family way and wants something done for her to get rid of it.
>
> Dr Townsend said he had told her nothing could be done for her and that he felt certain if she saw me I should tell her the same thing. I went into the dining room and found Mrs Schummacher there. She told me the same story, that she believed she was in the family way and asked me if I could help her to get rid of it. I told her most certainly I could not, that no

Doctor would hear of such a thing and that she must not suggest such a thing to me – I never mentioned the name of Dr Tarrico to her on that or any other occasion, nor did I say that if she went to him and he passed an instrument I would then take up the case – I did not see her again until Monday the 11th June, when I was told she was in the dining room - in my dining room. I went in and found her there and she again asked me if I would help her and I again told her I would not.

Dr Gloster's claims are the antithesis of those put forward by Eliza Schummacher and her sister Emily. Each should be treated with caution. The ladies' identification of the person referring Eliza to Dr Tarrico in the first instance is, as we have seen, ambiguous. It is not clear from 'he said go to Dr Tarrico' exactly who 'he' was. For his part Dr Gloster denies both making the referral and mention of Tarrico's name. However, he says nothing about accompanying Eliza Schummacher to Tarrico's premises himself, something he could easily have done without explicit prior reference. 'Allow me to introduce you to a colleague for a second opinion' is not exactly the equivalent of 'Go to Dr Tarrico!'

One must also bear in mind both the clinical and timing constraints imposed by Dr Bond, suggesting the patient's impaired mobility within 24 hours of an injury occurring between one and three weeks prior to death ("I hardly think three weeks"). Eliza Schummacher passed away on the night of June 27th. Monday the 18th, the date of Eliza's conspicuous invalidity, and one to which we shall return, was nine days prior; Monday the 11th all of sixteen days and just, therefore, within Dr Bond's hypothesized timescale. Monday the 4th was beyond three weeks. Eliza Schummacher complained of having been painfully violated by Dr Gloster on the 4th and the 11th when, according to her sister, she was perfectly mobile on June 8th and still working normally on the morning of the 16th.

Is it possible both versions are true - that Dr Gloster perhaps performed painful (though not fatal) examinations on two separate occasions, as Eliza Schummacher testified, and that the real damage was done subsequently, after yet another visit to Tarrico's Wardour Street practice, when she was accompanied by Dr Gloster himself?

CHAPTER 8

HOUSE CALLS

Following the original line of inquiry, we ought now to turn our attention to the weekend commencing 16th June and events immediately thereafter. Emily Maud Baker's recall to the witness stand highlights the significance of this period, although the reliability of her evidence is again open to question:

> She (ES) told me when she was ill she went to Dr Gloster on the Monday before Dr Gloster came on the 18th. I didn't see Dr Gloster on the 18th. She never gave me a description of a visit to Dr Gloster's house.

(Whose description, then, did this witness recount previously when she said, "When she was ill I questioned my sister who she had had and she told me. She said she had been to Dr Gloster at his house", etc.?)

> She told me when I went to Dr Gloster's on the 20th, I think, about Dr Gloster coming on the 18th...On Saturday the 16th she appeared perfectly well and made no complaint.

Despite the good doctor's protestations, we must at least entertain the possibility of his and/or others' visiting Eliza Schummacher at her time of distress, perhaps even being the cause of it. It was witness Mary Hull, giving evidence before

Magistrate L.T. d'Eyncourt, who opened a real can of worms, identifying Dr Gloster within it at the same time:

> I am wife of Charles Hull a coachman, since Christmas I have lived at 21 Moreton Place. I remember deceased dying on Wednesday. On Monday week (18th), before she died, I recollect her coming down into the kitchen. I believe it was about 2.30 to 3. It was after 2. I really couldn't say what time it was. She came down for a jug of hot water. Mrs Ambler, a lodger, was in the room. She asked for a jug of water, took it and went upstairs. I went into the front kitchen, my room, and sat there doing needlework. *A short time after, I heard the street door close. I looked up and saw someone leaving the house.* It was an hour or more after deceased asked for hot water. *Defendant was the person, or very like him.*
>
> He went towards Victoria – I don't know how he was dressed. I didn't notice if he had a hat on. I don't know what sort of hat.
>
> On the next day (Tuesday 19th) I was in the same room in the afternoon, sometime after 2. I couldn't say what time it was. I heard the street door shut very loud. It was slammed. *It was the same gentleman left that I saw on Monday. The same gentleman. That gentleman –*
>
> Since the death of the deceased I was brought to the Police Court and was shown a number of persons, twelve or more, I can't say exactly – I saw prisoner and spoke to Mr

Barnes. (note: this witness has earlier picked Gloster out of a line-up.)

My sight is very good. I can see quite clearly.

(Cross-examined):

On the Sunday after she died I was first asked if I could identify the person I saw.

Mr Barnes spoke to me (30th) before the inquest. I went to the inquest. When I was called to identify, I knew Dr Gloster had been arrested on Monday after the death. I knew he had been arrested. I didn't come to the Police Court. I saw the witnesses after they came from the court and I spoke to them about it. I was summoned to go to the inquest. I did go but was not called as a witness. The kitchen is below the level of the street, the window looks out on an area surrounded by walls. The area is one and a half yards wide I believe. It may be more. There is no table in front of the window. The area is not covered with a grating. There are iron railings to the area. I was sitting sideways looking toward the street door. I turned quite round when I heard the door go. I had been facing the door when I heard it I turned quite round. I can't see the front door. Victoria Station was at my back.

I never had seen the man before. He didn't interest me in the least.

On Monday I wasn't watching in the least. I saw him for a few seconds then. I have no idea how he was dressed or what sort of hat he had on.

It was on Monday and Tuesday as well I turned right round. On Monday the door shut quite quietly. The man walked fast away. He was coming with his face towards me. There is a door step and one step to the railings. Men would take 5 or 6 steps I think to get past the window. I went on with my work. I can't say if the man had an umbrella or stick in his hand.

On the Tuesday I didn't particularly watch. I heard the door slam. I was working then. The man went away towards Victoria Station.

I said to Mr Barnes that he was a fair man. I saw that on Monday and Tuesday. I am sure it was the same man on both days. When I came to identify I didn't put up my hand to another. I said of defendant I think this is the man.

There were other fair men there. There was no other man that even for an instant I thought was the man. I had been at the Police Courts on the different remands.

I think it was the first time I came here I picked him out.

I know Mrs Burles. I have seen her at the Police Court. I didn't know she had spoken to Dr Gloster on the Tuesday. I have heard the telegraph spoken of since but I didn't know. I sit much at the window *I have not seen any men go in – the people have latchkeys. I have seen a gentleman once call. Gilbert.* But I don't know his name. I am sometimes sitting at the window after 7. One evening in the winter time I let Mrs Schummacher in with a gentleman. I have not seen people leave the house – I don't know much of what goes on upstairs.

Recalled:

I don't know if the gentleman I let in was Gilbert.

There is one step from the door to the slab. I don't think any from the slab to the pavement. I sat looking toward the street door. I heard it and turned round – I don't know whether I got off the chair or not. I turned round so that I could have the better look I could see a person passing the house without turning right round – I should have to turn to see him go past as he came and he faced me.

There are I think about twelve steps into the area. I watched on Tuesday. Something had occurred which made me take notice.

I am quite certain it was not Mr Statham who came out on the Monday or Tuesday.

(signed) Mary Hull

Mary Hull's apparent identification of Dr Gloster as someone she saw leaving Eliza Schummacher's premises on both the Monday *and* Tuesday afternoons (18th and 19th June around 3.00 p.m.), is obviously an important consideration. There are others. It should be noted also that Mary Hull's *unequivocal* identification of Gloster is in fact reserved for the Tuesday, when she 'took notice', after hearing the street door slam shut. On the Monday it closed quietly and her attention was not therefore drawn to the 'fair man', in whom she was not interested and who passed before the window in just a few seconds, neither wearing a hat nor carrying a cane as far as the witness was able to recall. Despite her forthright equation of the gentleman seen on Tuesday with the one seen on the Monday, her earlier '*Defendant was the person or very like him*' opens the door to uncertainty somewhat. (We shall soon see it opened wider still with the testimony of Mrs Burles.)

By "the people have latch keys" Mrs Hull means, we must suppose, the upstairs lodgers. She did not see *men* go in, but she did once witness a Mr Gilbert (whose name she did not know, yet used in court). Nor had she seen people leave the house (having just carefully described Dr Gloster's doing so). Sometimes to be found at the window after 7.00 p.m., she once, in winter, opened the door to Mrs Schummacher and a gentleman whom she could not afterwards identify as Mr Gilbert, raising the possibility of there being at least three male visitors to her certain knowledge. Her claim that she didn't know much of what went on upstairs conversely suggests that something *did* go on, although she professed ignorance of it.

It is obvious where this line of defence questioning was going. Mary Hull, on returning to the witness stand, reaffirmed her purposeful behaviour:

> I watched on Tuesday. Something had occurred which made me take notice.

She then volunteered a little extra:

> *I am quite certain it was not Mr Statham who came out on the Monday or Tuesday.*

Where did that name come from? Wherever it was, and we shall discover it ere long, it brings the tally of identified male visitors now to four.

At this point it is pertinent we recall Dr Gloster's earlier explanation to Inspector Burner of Eliza Schummacher's accusatory behaviour:

You don't know her. She is a bad, drunken woman.

We have of course already seen how Eliza's sisters denied any suggestion that she was anything other than sober in her habits, but what, exactly, did Gloster mean when he described her as 'bad'? Clearly, distinguishing between 'bad' and 'drunk', as Gloster did, leaves little room for the imagination. An incident yet to be discussed removes all doubt in that regard, but first we need to hear more about the comings and goings witnessed at 21 Moreton Place that Monday and Tuesday, this time from Mrs Burles.

This is her signed witness statement (a second account, given in court, follows this one):

> Elizabeth Burles wife of Henry William
> Burles, freeman baker 27 Aylesford Place
> Pimlico. Sworn saith:
>
> I was in the employ of the deceased from the Thursday week before ten. Tuesday I spoke to the doctor. I had not known her before I answered an advertisement in the paper. She went out on the Monday before I had the interview with the doctor. She came home after I had come back from dinner. She came to the work room on the 2nd floor. She had two parlours below. I did not notice anything then. She said she had been called to a Lady somebody about some work. She said she had been to Kensington. I asked her if she would have some tea. She said she would as she hadn't had anything to eat.
>
> Mrs Schummacher went downstairs.

The apprentice went down and came back
& said, 'What is Mrs Schummacher dressing for
she is working herself.'

The child went downstairs again.

She came back.

The bell rang.

Mrs Schummacher went and opened it.
We waited a long time. We had our tea. During
the time we had our tea there was a lot of water
slopping about. Presently, after we had gone
into the workroom, Mrs Schummacher came
up to the top of the stairs and went into the back
room where we had been having our tea. She
called out, "Mrs Burles I want you a moment."

I went in and saw she was looking very bad.
She took a chair and sat in front of the fire and
said, "Oh my God, what have they done?"

I said, "What do you mean?"

She said, "Oh I do feel so bad, I could not
tell you."

She walked downstairs with me. She went
and got into bed. She was in her dressing gown.

I didn't see or hear any more but I heard
someone ring. About half-an-hour elapsed
before she came up. She came up during the
time we were having tea and asked for the
wadding. She said she had found it and went
downstairs again. When I went downstairs I did
not notice anything. I did not see anything
disarranged. I did not see the cotton wool. It
was ordinary white padding.

Mrs Schummacher was taken faint. When she came upstairs I never noticed anything about her health. She said she had had a fistula and hoped it was not coming back again.

She went about actively before this visit. The water was drawn on the drawing room floor.

On the next day I saw Mrs Schummacher when I went at 8.30 a.m. I asked her how she was. She said, "Oh I am in great pain."

I said, "Why don't you have someone else in to you?"

The Sunday night she said her doctor had been to her. She did not mention his name. She did not say he had done anything. I asked where he lived and she would send a telegram directly, because if you say it's inflammation you cannot be left here to die.

She said on Monday "I am in such pain it seems more like inflammation. She said then (on Tuesday), "I wish <u>you</u> could go and send a telegram."

She gave the name

Dr Gloster

High Street Kensington.

"Come to Norton Place at once."

I sent the telegram and wrote it. She dictated it. She could not write. I saw a doctor when I went. I went downstairs about 3 o'clock on Tuesday. I saw a hat & stick on the parlour table. I did not go into the bedroom. I stayed because I felt anxious. I accosted Dr Gloster as he came out and held my hand in the door of the parlour. He is the gentleman I identified yesterday morning at the Police Court.

I said, "You are the doctor. I should like to know what is the matter with Mrs Schummacher?"

He said, "It is nothing."

I said, "Remember I am a married woman and according to my suspicion I believe there is something. It is a very funny thing for a doctor to go into the room without another female present."

Dr Gloster said, "What makes you think it? You have never seen me before have you?"

I said, "No."

I said, "I believe it is more like a confinement."

He said, "Wait a minute. I'll go back and inquire."

He went back alone to Mrs Schummacher's room and shut the door. He came back not many minutes after and said, "I believe it is a menstruation now." He said she could have a hot bath and hot temperature flannels.

He went away. There was no vehicle outside. That was the last I saw of him. I saw nothing in the room. On the Wednesday I saw Mrs Schummacher in bed in the middle of the day.

She said, "I wish you came in here before you stopped that man."

I asked why. I said I could not go back again to see. I did not go back – She said nothing else. I did not like being spoken to in that manner. Doctors normally have another female with them when they examined female patients. She told me she had fistula the week before, as she was working the machine. I believed it. I never spoke to any doctor myself. I was standing some time in the hall.

(signed) E. Burles

And in court, under questioning:

<u>Elizabeth Burles</u> sworn.

I am wife of Henry William Burles I live at 54 North Street Sloane Street.

I knew deceased Mrs Schummacher.

I went into her Employment at 21 Moreton Place. It was Thursday fortnight or three weeks before I spoke to the prisoner. I didn't sleep in the house. I went from day to day to work. I was there on Monday before I left on Wednesday (the 20th) (margin note: on reading corrected to Thursday) the week before she died. I first noticed she was ill on Monday (the 18th). I had come back from dinner about 3. She came back about ¼ to 4. I noticed first that she was unwell. She came upstairs into the back room 2nd floor where we take meals. She looked very bad she took a chair and put it in front of the fire. She said "Oh my God what have they done? I feel so bad" – she had her dressing gown on – I went downstairs with her – I saw her go into the works room. There is wadding kept in that room for ladies dresses.

I saw her take some cotton wool from the cupboard and take it down with her. To my knowledge she did. She went straight downstairs into her bedroom. I didn't see her go in. I didn't that day go down with her. She went down that Monday alone. That was before she called me – I saw her go down on the Monday when she felt faint she went down stairs and I did so. She said "I feel so bad" she said outside the bedroom.

I remained with her till my time for going away. I left her about 8.30. She was still ill and complained of violent pain. I went home – on Tuesday I got to her house soon after 8. I went in her bedroom, she was in bed still in pain, she complained of violent pains internally. On that morning (Tuesday) I wrote the telegram produced at her request and dictation. That would be between 9 and 10.

I took it out to send it. I went to her sister's for the money and sent the telegram off.

I went home to dinner came back about 2 p.m., about 2.30 I saw the prisoner in Mrs Schummmacher's parlour. It was between 2 and 3 (on the Tuesday). There was a folding door – I took the chop in and I saw a stick and hat on the table. I waited and saw him come from the bedroom. He came from the passage into the room. I didn't know him before – I said, 'you're the doctor I believe' or 'are you the doctor?' He said, 'yes.' I said, 'I should like to know what is the matter with Mrs Schummacher.' He said, 'Oh, she'll be alright in a few days it's inflammation I believe.' I said, 'Remember Sir I am a married woman and it seems to me more than inflammation, she seems to be in such dreadful pain. It seems more like a premature confinement.' He said, 'Wait a minute I'll go back and see.' He went through the folding door into the bedroom. He was away not many minutes.

He came back, said 'Oh she'll be alright in a few days I believe it's only inflammation after all. Look after her well.' I said, 'Don't you think she had better have a nurse?' He said, 'Yes certainly.' I said, 'What should she have to eat?' He said, 'Oh, give her anything.' I said, 'I have just been cooking a chop for her.' He said, 'Yes she may have that, a hot bath and hot temperature flannels on the stomach.' When he told me this I didn't notice if the folding door was open – nothing more passed at that time. He left the house. The parlour is the front room. I didn't notice if there was anything at the door – I saw Mrs Schummacher till about 8 Sunday night. She was in bed. She had had a hot bath. Mrs Baker and I assisted – On Wednesday I again saw her. She was in bed, ill, and in pain.

I stayed till about midday – On Thursday morning I went again. She was still in bed. On that day I left at dinner time and did not return till Saturday 23rd and didn't see her after.

She never told me the name of the illness she was suffering from. The week previous she said she thought she had 'fistula'.

What we should be concerned to observe here are not the slight variations in Burles' two presentations of her evidence, but the relationship between her testimony and that of Mary Hull.

Mrs Burles describes seeing Dr Gloster on the Tuesday afternoon (the 19th), having previously sent him a telegram on Mrs Schummacher's behalf. Gloster himself admitted to having responded, however reluctantly, to that instruction. But Mrs Burles also describes noticing how Mrs Schummacher was unwell late on the Monday afternoon, around 4.00 p.m., after she had 'come back' from visiting a 'Lady somebody or other' in Kensington. Furthermore, in her deposition, she describes hearing the doorbell ring afterwards, followed by Mrs Schummacher moving up- and downstairs for water, wadding etc. in due course. Importantly Mrs Burles did not interact with anyone from outside the house staff that Monday. She encountered Dr Gloster, his hat and his cane, on the *Tuesday* afternoon. That is why Mr Gill paid so much attention to whether Mary Hull remembered seeing a gentleman leave the house wearing a hat and/or carrying a cane on either day. She did not.

The 'Lady somebody or other' Mrs Schummacher said she visited in Kensington on the Monday was, in all likelihood, Dr James Gloster, who, though he may not have done so in either his book or his 'lists', records her visit in his own statement to the court. While this invites us to consider the possibility of reciprocity on his part later that day, it also places a question mark against Eliza Schummacher's credibility. Was her 'white lie' to Elizabeth Burles simply to shield herself from any unwelcome inquisitiveness that might have ensued, or an indication of basic dishonesty?

The crux of the matter resides in who, exactly, visited Mrs Schummacher at her home late that Monday afternoon. Was it indeed Dr Gloster, as Mary Hull would have the court believe, or was he 'blind-sided' by another male medic of Eliza's acquaintance? Perhaps she was simply visited by a man friend, since neither the observant Mrs Burles nor the more casual Mary Hull noticed a 'Gladstone bag' on the Monday *or* the Tuesday. Dr Gloster may literally have had blood on his hands that Tuesday afternoon, having described the patient to Mrs Burles as menstruating. The real question, however, is whose hands, if any, were bloodied on the Monday?

One or other of the protagonists was clearly not playing with a straight bat. Perhaps some further evidence as to 'character' can help determine which.

CHAPTER 9

'COME AT ONCE!'

In answer to the charge laid against him, and with Dr Louis Tarrico having been discharged by the magistrate early on, Doctor James Gloster's statement to court amounts to the matter-of-fact story of his professional relationship with the deceased, as told by one voice, rather than assembled from diverse witness accounts. That does not identify it as either complete or entirely accurate however.

STATEMENT OF THE ACCUSED

James Gloster

(hereinafter called the Accused) stands charged before the undersigned, one of the Magistrates of the Police Courts of the Metropolis sitting at the Westminster Police Court in the Metropolitan Police District, this 16th day of August in the Year of our Lord One Thousand Eight Hundred and Eighty-eight as herein before set forth, and the said charge being read to the said Accused, and the said Witnesses for the prosecution being severally examined in the presence of the said Accused, the said Accused is now addressed by means as follows:

Having heard the evidence do you wish to say anything in answer to the charge? You are not obliged to say anything unless you desire to do so, but whatever you say will be taken down in writing and may be given in evidence against you upon your trial, and if you desire to call any Witness, you can now do so.

Whereupon the said Accused saith as follows:

I am not guilty and I desire to state fully all I know about the deceased – I recollect attending a child of the deceased woman between 3 and 4 years ago. I did not see her again until the evening of the fifth of June last when on going home late my friend and neighbour Dr Townsend who had been called in by one of my servants told me *a patient was in the dining room and had said she was in the family way and wants something done for her to get rid of it.*

Dr Townsend said he had told her nothing could be done for her and that he felt certain if she saw me I should tell her the same thing. I went into the dining room and found *Mrs Schummacher there. She told me the same story,* that she believed she was in the family way and asked me if I could help her to get rid of it. I told her most certainly I could not, that no Doctor would hear of such a thing and that she must not suggest such a thing to me. *I never mentioned the name of Dr Tarrico to her on that or any other occasion, nor did I say that if she went to him and he passed an instrument I would then take up the case.* I did not see her again until *Monday the 11th June*, when I was told she was in the dining room - in my dining room. I went in and found her there *and she* *again asked me if I would help her and I again told her I would not. I did not on this occasion ask her to change a cheque for me at Mr Buckle's.*

The piece of paper which has been produced (marked B) was written for the purpose of being taken over by one of my servants and Mrs Schummacher must have picked it up in the room while waiting for me. *I was told that she called again at my house on the night of Sunday 17ᵗʰ of June, accompanied by a little boy, and that she was coming the following evening to see me.* She did not come the next morning before I went out and when I returned rather late for luncheon I was told she was waiting in the dining room (the afternoon of Monday 18ᵗʰ), I went into the room taking one of my servants with me. I told her I was very much surprised to see her there again after I had told her from the first that I would have nothing to do with her. She implored me to help her and said if I did not she would be ruined. I told her I would have nothing to do with her and that she must be good enough to leave the house, and she did so, after an interval of a minute or two.

The following day I went out (margin note: Tuesday June 19ᵗʰ) rather early in the morning and did not return until after much time *when I found a telegram which I could not make out and which was unsigned.* During lunch I considered the telegram and saw that the office where it had been handed in was near the street where deceased had told me she was still living. Remembering that she had been a patient of mine and that *she might possibly be seriously ill*, I considered that I was bound, as a medical man at any rate, to go and see what was the matter. I went and walked along Moreton Place until I saw her name on a brass plate on the side of the door and was admitted by an elderly woman. I was shown into the deceased's bedroom and asked her if and why she had telegraphed me.

She said that she was in great pain and asked me if I could do anything for her. I asked her what her symptoms were and when she told me I said I thought she had inflammation and that as I could not attend her myself she had better either send for a medical man or go to the hospital. She said she wouldn't do this and pressed me to attend her. I told her I could not possibly do so and afterwards left the house.

On this occasion I saw the witness Burles, who smelt strongly of spirits, as did also the deceased. *I did not go to the house on the previous day nor did either on the 11th or 17th June or on any other day use any instruments or do anything to her of any kind whatever.* I did not attend the inquest because my solicitor told me the enquiry could not possibly be concluded that day and it would not have been finished that evening but for the fact that a change was being made in the office of Coroner.

That is my statement.

(signed) James Gloster MB MCh

(signed) Taken before me as aforesaid

L.T. d'Eyncourt

This account arouses suspicion at several junctures. Dr Gloster 'asked what her symptoms were' and 'thought she had inflammation', although he would have been well aware already of Mrs Schummacher's imminent objective. Having been told of Mrs Schummacher's intention to pay a return visit 'the following *evening*', why should Gloster have been careful to negate her attendance 'the next *morning* before he went out'?

After first puzzling over the telegram, he eventually decides to 'go and see what was the matter' (as if he didn't know), remembering 'that she might possibly be seriously ill'.

How might a woman become 'seriously ill' within 24 hours of bemoaning her possible pregnancy? Dr Gloster's statement at this point appears to be placing a considerable distance between his last personal recollection of the patient's attendance, in the company of her young son (overlooking their more recent interactions completely), and newly developed clinical symptoms on her part, of which he is wholly unaware. It is evasive.

Perhaps it was discretion then that led the doctor to observe simply, 'he could not attend her', without further explaining why not.

The incident deserving of most careful scrutiny however is that of the (Tuesday) telegram, Eliza Schummacher having called at the doctor's surgery on both Sunday *and* Monday, according to this account.

> During lunch I considered the telegram and saw
> that the office where it had been handed in was
> near the street where deceased had told me she
> was still living.

This would suggest Dr Gloster did not know Mrs Schummacher's exact address at that precise moment in time, i.e., that he had not visited recently. Described as a reflection of his professional duty, Gloster's response appears both laudable and innocuous.

Emily Maud Baker on the other hand saw it somewhat differently. Earlier in the case (17th July) she deposed, *inter alia*:

> On *Wednesday 20th* before 11 a.m. from what my sister said I went to the defendant's. Dr James Gloster 15 Upper Phillimore Place was the address given me – I rang the bell, was shown in and saw prisoner. I said, 'I've come from my sister Mrs Schummacher and she has asked me to ask you to come to her as she is very ill.' He said, 'No, I won't come. I would not come to your sister again. She has deceived me. She sent a telegram by that woman with my name on, open in full. I wouldn't come if you were to lay me down £500 this minute. *I won't be seen in the neighbourhood again* – my name is my name.' I said, 'what am I to do?' He said, 'You go back to your sister and tell her to send you to Dr Tarrico and say she is in great pain, and she had got a show and that he would come to her alone and charge her two guineas.' He told me not to come near his house again. That is all that passed as far as I remember.

If this account of Emily Maud's is in any way accurate, it provides observations of considerable significance in this case; observations attributed to Dr Gloster himself.

The medical man would neither visit the patient *again* nor indeed be 'seen again in the neighbourhood', both of which protestations confirm his having done so on at least one occasion previously. Whether or not Eliza was justified in claiming he visited her on the Monday, and independently of Mary Hull's 'identification', it has to be accepted that a visit on the Tuesday alone would qualify him just as readily to state his case as he did.

Now what of 'deception'?

It is a moot point whether Eliza deceived Dr Gloster by arranging for him to receive her telegram, or whether the deception and the telegram were, in fact, separate actions, in which case one might be obliged to speculate as to the nature of the former. Whatever the situation, Mrs Schummacher was upbraided for sending a telegram by 'that woman'; a condescending reference, no doubt to Mrs Burles, who, together with Mrs Schummacher, was said to have been smelling of spirits when Dr Gloster paid his Tuesday afternoon visit.

Even if we allow Eliza Schummacher the benefit of the doubt, conclude that Dr Gloster was mistaken in his judgement of her, and accept that she had simply been given some gin by Emily Maud 'for medicinal purposes', the question mark against Mrs Burles, who denied any knowledge of the gin at all, remains.

Burles at least admitted to having been downstairs on several occasions, where the gin was kept 'at times'. Is it not likely that temptation will have come her way? With Eliza seriously indisposed might she not have thought, "Well, whilst I'm here...."? Dr Gloster must surely have had some grounds for emphasising the otherwise anonymous woman who authored the (unsigned) telegram. Having referred to an intermediary, he must also have had grounds for understanding that Eliza Schummacher did not despatch it personally. Worse yet, the telegram bore his name 'open in full'. So dire was this action that Dr Gloster could not be bribed into returning, even for more than a year's salary!

Dr Thomas Bond (author unknown – Obituary of
Dr Thomas Bond - The Lancet, 1901 Vol. I, p. 1721).

Mr (later Sir) Charles
Frederick Gill - defence
counsel for Dr James Gloster.
©Victoria and Albert
Museum, London.

Mr (later Sir) Harry Bodkin
Poland – counsel for
the prosecution,
Regina vs. Gloster.
©Victoria and Albert
Museum, London.

Wardour Street, Soho. No.22, formerly the practice whereabouts of Dr Louis Tarrico and since occupied by a Chinese restaurant, is to the left of picture. Author's copyright.

Upper Phillimore Place, Kensington. Nowadays considered part of Kensington High Street. Author's copyright.

Moreton Place, Pimlico. No.7 the birthplace of William Morris Hughes (later to become Prime Minister of Australia). Elizabeth Schummacher lived at No.21. Author's copyright.

A portico at Moreton Place, Pimlico. The door to no.21, last home of Elizabeth Schummacher, is to the viewer's left. Author's copyright.

The Lusk letter. Author unknown. Original in the Records of Metropolitan Police Service, National Archives, MEPO 3/142 (this facsimile from http://www.casebook.org/ripper_letters/).

The Lusk letter, as if signed by Henry G.A.S. Statham.

Map of the Whitechapel area
(Reynolds, 1882. Courtesy of Birkbeck History Dept.).

What aspect of Eliza's deception was so grave, or characteristic of the neighbourhood so undesirable, as to jeopardize Dr Gloster's good name by association? The sender and recipient were known to each other were they not?

The root cause of this tirade was possibly the fact that the former party was known to others besides. Whether this person was Eliza Schummacher or the opportunistically inebriate Mrs Burles, whoever had sight of the telegram at the point of despatch would have been in a position to 'put two and two together'. 'Come at once – Moreton', which is all it said, reads as a directive, not a request. Even allowing brevity for the sake of economy, omission of the word 'Please' lends an altogether different character to the narrative.

There is no reason why anyone with, shall we say, background knowledge, should assume the instruction necessarily pertained to a medical emergency. If Eliza Schummacher or Elizabeth Burles had a reputation in the area for anything other than needlework, this could easily have led to someone's drawing an inappropriate conclusion from the telegram in question.

Unduly or otherwise, Dr Gloster was clearly very sensitive regarding perceived associations between himself, Eliza Schummacher, Elizabeth Burles, and 21 Moreton Place, Pimlico. Yet there is a simpler, darker explanation for his alarmed reaction to the telegram; one which casts a shadow, not over the good residents of Moreton Place so much as upon Dr Gloster himself.

We have seen that, for some reason, Dr Gloster discounts Monday morning as a point in time when he and Mrs Schummacher might have met, despite there having been no intimation on the patient's part of any intended assignation until the evening. We know also that Dr Tarrico entertained Dr Gloster, together with a female patient-friend, prior to Tuesday the 19th. Not only did he describe them as arriving together, they left together also ('He went away with the patient').

Despite, shall we say, the 'element of doubt', which the defence counsel succeeded in introducing into the various eye-witness testimonies recorded on behalf of the prosecution, it is by no means beyond the realm of possibility that it was indeed Mrs Schummacher who accompanied Dr Gloster to Tarrico's Wardour Street practice, and who remained in his company afterwards. What might they have spoken about? What might they have arranged? And, playing devil's advocate, if the doctor finally relented and eventually attended the patient in the manner specified, what might they have agreed upon? Anonymity perchance?

Imagine someone in Dr Gloster's position having their name publicly revealed in the immediate aftermath of a private visit, following which it might be discovered, through neighbourhood gossip perhaps, that the patient had coincidentally been 'cured' of a rather particular personal problem. They could suddenly acquire a reputation in the area that would expose them to accusations of felony. However sought after such skills might then become, it would be difficult to exercise them profitably from inside Pentonville or other prison.

Could this have been the nature of the deceit which Doctor Gloster found so offensive? The idea receives support from a strange 'aside' which he is said to have made to Mrs Burles whilst at the house on the Tuesday afternoon:

You have never seen me before have you?

Bearing in mind that this question was put on the premises, so to speak, it can hardly reflect a concern for what the 'neighbourhood' might imagine was Dr Gloster's purpose or remit. He is clearly aware here of appearances inside the house, not outside, and in connection therefore with matters immediately to hand, not the least of which being Eliza Schummacher's state of health. Had Dr Gloster never visited previously, the occupants of no. 21 would, perforce, have been strangers to him, and the question simply redundant. That he chose to ask it reflects a concern that he not be recognised or identified as a prior visitor, which in turn implies that he had been.

This is of course conjecture, but a closing aspect of Dr Gloster's statement is anything but. Speaking of Tuesday the 19th, he says:

> On this occasion I saw the witness Burles who smelt strongly of spirits, as did also the deceased. *I did not go to the house on the previous day nor did either on the 11th or 17th June or on any other day use any instruments or do anything to her of any kind whatever.*

The second claim here suffers on account of what might be described as the overworked 'not'.

Without hearing the words spoken, and for want of punctuation, the exact meaning could be open to question. On the one hand it might seem a categorical denial regarding the use of an instrument on any day at all, including those specifically referred to. There is a rather different interpretation available to us however.

The accused *does not say*, "I did not, on any day (i.e., any day at all), use any instruments..." Instead he first locates three dates (the 18th, 11th, and 17th June), whereafter the remainder of the statement could be interpreted as denying malpractice on any other (i.e., *remaining*) day, or a visitation on any of the three days specified. Dr Gloster's meaning would be altogether clearer had the clerk of the court but inserted a comma, either following the phrase, 'the previous day', or immediately after the word 'June', neither of which amendments could have ruled out the doctor's *use of an instrument* on the 18th, the crucial Monday.

Unfortunately we are not assisted in our understanding by Dr Gloster's description of Mrs Schummacher's calling upon *him* at various times on various days, when she herself is reported by Mrs Burles to have said that on the Sunday night (17th June) 'her doctor had been to her'. Eliza, as we have seen, was keener to refer to visits paid *to her* than *by her*.

Emily Baker's being made aware of the envelope fragment as 'proof' of Dr Gloster's visit on the 11th is unconvincing when one considers that the message written upon it would have been better communicated in the immediate environs of Upper Phillimore Place (where the obliging postmaster was situated) than at Moreton Place, some distance (and a considerable walk) away.

Someone, we are told, called (again?) quietly on the Monday, and the accused conspicuously on the Tuesday. But who was that someone? And did they really call at all?

The nonchalant Mary Hull, not terribly interested in the man she saw leave Mrs Schummacher's premises on the Monday afternoon, fixes the visitor's departure at some time after 2.00 p.m., placing it alongside her interaction with lodger Louise Ambler, who had come all the way downstairs for some water. Louise Ambler herself recalls a similar moment – on the Tuesday. Mary Hull's words once more (see chapter 5):

> On Monday week before she died I recollect
> her coming down into the kitchen. I believe it
> was about 2.30 to 3. It was after 2. I really
> couldn't say what time it was - She came down
> for a jug of hot water. Mrs Ambler, a lodger, was
> in the room (etc.)

And Louise Ambler's:

> The day (she means week) before she died on
> a Tuesday the 19th I remember drawing some
> water on the landing between the dining and

> drawing room floor. It was some time I think
> between 1 and 3, (etc.)

Might these two ladies have actually been describing the same incident, occurring on the same day, Tuesday the 19th?

Dr Gloster's final word on the matter, according to Emily Maud at least, was for her to return to her sister and tell *her* to send Emily to Dr Tarrico and say she was in great pain.

This is where the pendulum swings, once again, toward Dr Gloster's knowing rather more about the events than he seems prepared to admit, having said of his previous personal interactions with Eliza Schummacher:

> I never mentioned the name of Dr Tarrico to
> her on that or any other occasion.

If Gloster had 'never mentioned the name of Dr Tarrico' to his patient at all, then what reaction did he expect her sister Emily Maud to provoke when conveying the message that she, Eliza, should instruct her to go to Dr Tarrico on her behalf – 'Dr who?' He gives no further details to the bemused Emily, whom he has not previously met and cannot therefore imagine to have already been in possession of Tarrico's name and address. If he knew the sisters to have visited Tarrico independently of any referral on his part, he must either have reasoned that said referral had earlier originated with his own 'assistant', Dr Townsend, or been personally aware, at the very least, that such referral had already been made. In which case, why did he not say so in the first place?

It will be recalled that Dr Tarrico did not identify the patient whom Dr Gloster brought with him to Wardour Street seven, eight, nine or ten days before Tarrico himself was arrested. He did identify Dr Gloster though. What then would have been the chances of Dr Gloster's having *two* female patients that same week, each presenting with similar puzzling abdominal symptoms? Had Dr Gloster paid this visit to Tarrico on the Tuesday (19th), it could not have been in the company of Eliza Schummacher, who was literally crippled with pain come the Monday night.

If Dr Tarrico is to be believed therefore, Eliza Schummacher was escorted to Soho by Dr Gloster *no later than* Monday the 18th June. Eliza told of her visit to a 'Lady somebody' in Kensington that day, whilst Dr Gloster freely admits she called on *him*. Neither party, for differing reasons, was being perfectly candid.

According to Dr Gloster, Eliza departed his practice alone 'after an interval of a minute or two', having yet again failed to compromise his medical career (or had she?). Given her degree of desperation by this time, how might she then have secured the services of another doctor later that very same afternoon? To whom might she have turned that she had not already approached, obviously without success?

Is it at all likely that she closed Dr Gloster's door behind her, only to go immediately to another medical practitioner, of whatever complexion; one who was coincidentally free either to accompany or follow her home before 4 p.m. (the time of her upstairs encounter with Mrs Burles), having acceded to an illegal proposition beforehand? (Mrs Burles' account has Eliza showing signs of distress by this time.) Whoever this phantom may have been, they too will have had a collaborator, as Mrs Schummacher is quoted, again by Mrs Burles, to have exclaimed: "Oh my God! What have *they* done?"

Dr Gloster's defence would, of course, endeavour to explore these rather unlikely possibilities.

CHAPTER 10

A STELLAR WITNESS

First let us recall that closing comment of witness Mary Hull's:

> I am quite certain it was not Mr Statham who
> came out on the Monday or Tuesday.

To whom was this witness referring?

Henry George Algernon Sydney Statham, of Leighton, Essex (another doctor, or someone with medical training at least), became deliberately involved in the Schummacher case; that is to say he involved himself, having read the initial reports in the newspaper (or had them read to him). He too had an associate, a Dr Robertson, who, it was claimed, freely volunteered to him that he, Robertson, had attended the deceased.

Armed with this information, Dr Statham felt honour bound to 'get the poor beggar (Gloster) off'. He duly visited the Gloster household, where he spoke with a brother (most probably Thomas, a land valuer and captain of Militia over from Ireland) then afterwards to Dr James Gloster's solicitor, Mr Stokes. Whatever tales he told them (and we shall soon have them first-hand), he found himself subpoenaed as a witness, when his intention had been simply to denounce his acquaintance, Dr Robertson.

Nor was Mary Hull the only prosecution witness to be cross-examined regarding a relationship to, or knowledge of, Dr Henry Statham. Another of Eliza's sisters, Agnes Beresford gave a statement which included the following:

I didn't know that Gilbert visited the house, not until after the Friday Dr Crane was sent for. I didn't see Gilbert there. I know a man of the name of Hunt. He lives in Vauxhall Bridge Road. I don't know the number. I have known him for years. I have not lived in the house with the Hunts, but with his mother. I believe Hunt is a clerk to a solicitor. I know he is. *I don't know a man named Statham, not one called Dr Statham. I never heard of him.* I left the house in Vauxhall Bridge Road years ago. I have not been there since, not to that house. I lived in 200. I have been to the Hunts but never lived there. I have been there this year, not with Mrs Schummacher. I did not know any one at that house who passed as a doctor. *I didn't know any man named Statham. The gentleman pointed out to me as Dr Statham I never saw before till this day.* I knew both Miss Gardeners. I have seen them with Mrs Schummacher. I have not seen them at 158 Vauxhall Bridge Road. I don't know Miss Gardener's writing.

The Gardener sisters, Georgina and Fanny (Garwood), were themselves invited to identify this same intrusive witness. Georgina, under cross examination stated:

I only wrote about two letters, and they were business letters. *I do not know Dr Statham* – I never heard of his name before.

Fanny, however, had further questions to answer:

> *I don't know the name of Statham* – I don't know
> the writing nor the name on the Envelope produced.
>
> *I know no one passing by the name of Statham.*
>
> My sister at Southampton didn't know I was
> coming here.
>
> My sister Eugenie didn't know anything about
> *letters written to Dr Statham* – not my sister
> Eugenie. I have seen Dr S in the next room not
> spoken to him.
>
> Not any of my sisters knew anything of any letters.
>
> I don't see that the correspondence would
> interest them. Not about dress - I have not
> spoken to my sisters about a letter written to a
> Doctor for Mrs Schummacher, I swear that.

Is it not a strange thing that a witness, ostensibly for the defence,
should become the subject of interest during the cross-
examination of *four different* witnesses for the crown?

We must return to this development after hearing from Dr
Statham personally. He had rather a lot to say for himself, as we
shall have to discuss. Although cross-examined at the time, a more
detailed analysis of his shambling, erratic evidence is most
certainly called for. Herewith his first attempt:

> Henry George Algernon Sydney Statham sworn:
>
> I live at Birch Hill Cottage Leighton Essex. I am
> a gentleman. I have not any occupation. I have
> no place of business – I have had an
> occupation. I was in the army 10 years as an

officer. I am a Doctor of Medicine and Master in Surgery of the University of Pennsylvania. I qualified in 1873 for medicine and for surgery in 1874. I came to England in 1875. I have been living at my present address 15 months.

After Dr Gloster was charged in this case I went to his house. I saw his housekeeper first and then his brother. He referred me to Mr Stokes who is acting for Dr Gloster as solicitor.

I went to Mr Stokes offices I can't say the date. Mr Neville was with me and Dr Robertson. I don't know Dr Neville's address. He went to Darlington 3 or 4 weeks ago. He is like myself a ship's doctor. I mean I used to be.

Dr Robertson is I think of Maine USA. He *left England the day after I took the 2^{d} document to Mr Stokes,* that document which was copied by Mr Stokes' clerk.

The first occasion I went, I think I saw Mr Stokes. I gave the name of Statham. I gave my address at Mr Maynard's Solicitor of 12 Clifford Inn. That is where I have letters addressed as *Mr Maynard has frequent business with me.**

I did not ask Mr Stokes or his clerk what the punishment would be to a man who knew abortion had been procured and that the woman knew how to do it - I can't say if I stayed from 11.30 a.m. till ¼ to 4 p.m. I can't say I did. I don't know. I was not asked to bring a written statement. *Some day or another I went to Mr Stokes with a statement on half sheets of note paper.* I left them at his office either with Mr

Stokes or his clerk. I believe with Mr Stokes. I afterwards called again with a written statement and got back the sheets of note paper. *I got the sheets back before I brought the 2^{d} statement.* I have not got them. They were destroyed in my presence – they became worthless then. I can't say whether the paper produced is a copy or not.

I gave Mr Stokes what is written at the back. *The original letter I never had* – I afterwards called with another statement of which (3) is a press copy. *It was written by me at various places.* This is a facsimile of my writing.

I wrote part of the original at Maynard's office. No. 3 doesn't represent my evidence – I took it down from Dr Robertson. I believe he will be home shortly. I don't know what he may do after he gets my letter. I don't know what ship he went on. He went for New York said he was going to Boston I don't know if States of Maine or Massachusetts, but he generally hangs out in Maine. *He went about 2 days after I gave Mr Stokes the last statement.*

I don't know what ship he went by I think he went by Liverpool. I don't know what line. *I got a letter from him from Liverpool.* I destroyed it directly I read it. *I destroyed it the 2^{d} or 3^{d} day after I gave Stokes the statement produced.* I addressed as Dr Robertson Poste Restante New York. We call him Roger of that ilk. I don't know his real Christian name. I have kept no copy of my letter to him. *I didn't mention to him this case.* I thought he'd go on to 'Frisco. *I gave the original statement to Dr Robertson.*

He was a stout man about 5 ft. 9 or 10. A fair man.

He made the statement when he drew my attention to the newspaper. I said perhaps we can get the poor beggar off. Let's try.

I got the statements from Robertson at various times. *Neville is a relation of mine, and had nothing to do with the statement beyond conversation.*

I wrote Robertson if he went to 'Frisco and used my name he might get on there was the New Zealand and Panama line.

I never saw Mrs Schummacher in my life – I said to Robertson if that is right we can get the poor beggar off.

Robertson was residing in a lodging House in Gower Street. He told me so.

All the information, the full of it, is Robertson's. *I did not know anyone named Gardener. Yes I know Dr Gardener.*

I never knew anyone of that name write to me.

I brought a Barnes uterine sound and Freiberts uterine irrigator to (Dr Gloster's house – deleted) Mr Stokes' office. *I have got a lot of them in my possession.* I don't know Miss Gardener. I have seen some letters in connection with this case in the possession of Dr Robertson – one or two signed, I think, yours faithfully, Mrs Schummacher.

I told Mr Stokes I could give Robertson's name and address and said I thought he ought to have subpoenaed him. I didn't give his name and address. *I never had Mrs Schummacher's letters except a torn one a few hours.* The envelope produced addressed to me is written by a Miss Brady.

I understood and told Mr Stokes that that letter was written by someone who had worked for Mrs Schummacher. I have not the letter. I tore it up and kept the envelope.

Miss Brady is at Neuilly near Paris. She left London the end of July or beginning of August since this case came on. She has no address in London.

I have not in this matter been asking on the advice of a solicitor.

Yes I have been acting under Mr Stokes' advice giving him all the information I could.

I only acted on Mr Maynard's advice. He said I was a fool to enter into these matters.

I told Mr Stokes that I had heard there were certain instruments I could put him on the way of. I know nothing of my own knowledge.

I asked him to pay the men who had got the information for him when they called for it as a matter of fact I paid money out of my pocket and showed Mr Stokes the receipts. Mr Stokes wanted me to go on. I said yes but the men must be paid as they did the work. I didn't want to be paid. I paid Hanson, a general enquiry officer. I paid him in Chancery Lane – all together I paid nearly £4. There were two other receipts, one was Mary Bowse. I can't give the 3rd. I paid nearly £4 out of my own pocket to make enquiries into this case.

I should look about Chancery Lane for him. I never saw the two women.

The copy letter annexed I copied from one Dr Robertson had.

Until I saw the case in the paper I knew nothing of any of the parties. In July I didn't know where Miss Brady lived I never wrote to her she wrote to me.

I didn't know Robertson was going to leave till just before.

I destroyed Miss Brady's letter at once. I am here on Subpoena.

I have taken notes which you can look through – *I don't know Neville's address. He is in London, I can see him tonight. I wouldn't mind saying I did it myself to get the man off."*

Cross examined:

I have no practice. I have a pension. I was in the navy as midshipman in Pearl and enlisted in the mutiny in 1857. And I became Paymaster in 2nd Bengal and the 20th Hussars.
I became instructor of Musketry in 1859.
I was Lieutenant in the Worcestershire Militia.
I was Lieutenant in the army and Captain in the Company & Service. I can't say when I left the Militia. It was about 1869. I think 1868. I am not in the Employ of Mr Maynard. I have had cases for him. I have been in his employment getting up evidence. That is what I mostly do.

My pension is £47 a year. I have private income
in all about £250.

(handwritten in margin: 'Taken & sworn before me')

(Signed)   L.T. d'Eyncourt   Henry Statham

Now for some detailed scrutiny of Henry Statham's 'evidence' so far:

I live at Birch Hill Cottage Leighton Essex. I am a
gentleman. I have not any occupation. I have no
place of business – I have had an occupation. I
was in the army 10 years as an officer.

I was Lieutenant in the army and Captain in the
Company & Service.

Commissioned into the Worcestershire Militia in 1858, as an
Ensign, he resigned, without further promotion to Lieutenant, two
years later, in June 1860. The Company & Service he refers to is
the East India Company, which basically ran the Indian Army,
both before and after its nationalisation in 1858. Statham's answer
under cross-examination is no more accurate.

I am a Doctor of Medicine and Master in Surgery
of the University of Pennsylvania – I qualified in
1873 for medicine and for surgery in 1874.

The now defunct 'American University of Pennsylvania' - not to
be confused with the 'Department of Medicine of the University
of Pennsylvania'- is recognized as having been an illegal, fraudulent
organization, its medical alumni regarded as 'unregistered
practitioners'. It is by no means clear to which university 'Dr'
Statham was referring.

I went to Mr Stokes offices I can't say the date.
Mr Neville was with me and Dr Robertson.

Note here the representation by three, 'the liars' number' according to statement analysis practitioners in the USA.

> I don't know Dr Neville's address.

From being simply a 'Mr', Neville has suddenly become a doctor. Curiously, a Thomas Neville, of 85 Pimlico Road and 123 Sloane Street, was a Divisional Surgeon for the police at the time.

> He went to Darlington 3 or 4 weeks ago. He is
> like myself a ship's doctor. I mean I used to be.

Later he will say he was referring to Robertson here, *not* Neville. Statham claimed to have been a mere midshipman at the time of the Indian mutiny (1857). He did not qualify in medicine until sixteen years later, surgery the following year. In 1875 he left America for England. When did he serve as a ship's doctor in America therefore?

> The first occasion I went, I think I saw Mr
> Stokes. I gave the name of Statham.

What name might he have given otherwise?

> *Someday or another I went to Mr Stokes with a*
> *statement on half sheets of note paper.* I left
> them at his office either with Mr Stokes or his
> clerk. I believe with Mr Stokes.

This is rather indeterminate, given the seriousness of the matter at hand.

> I afterwards called again with a written
> statement and got back the sheets of note paper.
> *I got the sheets back before I brought the*
> *second statement.*

Suggesting he actually called again *twice* – or even thrice – more.

> I have not got them. They were destroyed in
> my presence.

Where, and by whom, given they were retrieved before presentation of the more formal second statement? This makes no sense.

> I gave Mr Stokes what is written at the back.
> *The original letter I never had.*

What letter? He's been talking about 'statements' – '*The original letter I never had.*' This is errant nonsense. If the envelope and its contents were delivered to him then he must have been in possession of both at some time.

> I wrote part of the original at Maynard's office.
> No. 3 doesn't represent my evidence – I took it
> down from Dr Robertson.

He wrote part of the original *what* at Maynard's office? The letter?

> I believe he will be home shortly.

How convenient is that?

> I don't know what he may do after he gets my letter.

Perhaps he'll elect to stay out of the country.

> I don't know what ship he went on. He went for
> New York, said he was going to Boston. I don't
> know if States of Maine or Massachusetts, but
> he generally hangs out in Maine. *He went about*
> *2 days after I gave Mr Stokes the last statement.*

Quelle surprise.

> I don't know what ship he went by. I think he
> went by Liverpool. I don't know what line. *I got*
> *a letter from him from Liverpool.* I destroyed it

> directly I read it. *I destroyed it the 2^d or 3^d day*
> *after I gave Stokes the statement produced.*

The Royal Mail was at a peak of efficiency toward the end of the 19th c., achieving several deliveries daily within the capital. 'Same day delivery' was perfectly possible across London therefore, but from Liverpool? Robertson went 'about 2 days after' Stokes was handed the last statement, whilst Statham here claims to have received and destroyed his last letter at exactly the same period in time; a letter most likely written *after* Robertson had left London, since it was posted from Liverpool, but before his departure for New York. He must have been away from the capital for several days, having first accompanied Statham on his initial visit to Mr Stokes' offices, which Statham visited at least once thereafter.

> He was a stout man about 5 ft. 9 or 10.

'*Was* a stout man'? Had he since died?

> I addressed as Dr Robertson Poste Restante
> New York. We call him Roger of that ilk. I
> don't know his real Christian name. I have kept
> no copy of my letter to him. *I didn't mention to*
> *him this case.* I thought he'd go on to 'Frisco. *I*
> *gave the original statement to Dr Robertson.*

Robertson is supposed to have mentioned the case to Statham in the first place, not *vice versa*. Nor did Statham earlier claim he 'gave the original statement to Dr Robertson'. He goes on to state that he got statements *from* him, not gave them *to* him.

> I told Mr Stokes I could give Robertson's name
> and address.

This must be the address he 'doesn't know', presumably.

> I never saw Mrs Schummacher in my life – I
> said to Robertson if that is right we can get the
> poor beggar off.

If *what* is right? That Robertson performed the surgery, or instructed the patient as to how she might accomplish it personally?

> Robertson was residing in a lodging House in
> Gower Street. He told me so. All the
> information, the full of it, is Robertson's.

What information? Not disclosed it would seem.

> I told Mr Stokes I could give Robertson's name
> and address.

Again, the address he 'doesn't know'.

> *Miss Brady is at Neuilly near Paris. She left*
> *London the end of July or beginning of August*
> *since this case came on.*

We have yet another coincidence.

> I told Mr Stokes that I had heard there were
> certain instruments I could put him on the way
> of finding.

Does he not keep a collection himself? Why the need for extras if so?

> I asked him to pay the men who had got the
> information for him.

What information?

> I said yes but the men must be paid as they did
> the work.

What work? All he's done so far is 'force' statements of Robertson's. How does that equate to 'work' done by hired hands?

> I paid nearly £4 out of my own pocket to make
> enquiries into this case.

Regarding what exactly?

> I should look about Chancery Lane for him.

For whom? Hanson, the general enquiry officer, presumably.

> *Until I saw the case in the paper I knew nothing*
> *of any of the parties.*

He earlier claimed it was Robertson who read of the case and drew his attention to it.

> I have taken notes which you can look through
> – *I don't know Neville's address. He is in*
> *London, I can see him tonight.*

Where, exactly, might he have expected to see Neville? By the late 19th c. London was already a very big city. How was he going to look him up without knowing the address?

> *I wouldn't mind saying I did it myself to get the*
> *man off.*

Whether confessing to a murder, or falsely confessing to a murder, the offence carried the death penalty either way, without a right to appeal. As the late Nick Warren, founding editor of 'Ripperana' has pointed out, this remark of Statham's directly refutes his statement to the Magistrate's Court, opening him up to a charge of provable perjury.

It will come as no surprise that Dr Henry Statham's testimony of the 20th August, on reading over his own evidence, is no more convincing than his first attempt:

> (20th August 1888)
>
> (margin note) Dr Statham on reading evidence
>
> I was 10 years in the army (the figure written looks conspicuously like 18) 4 years of which with the Queen's Commission.

He resigned the commission of Ensign after only two years. His tenure as a *commissioned* officer with the HEIC must have been equally short-lived therefore, rendering his earlier statement - "I was in the army 10 years as an officer" - open to question.

> Neville is not a ship's doctor. When I said he is like myself, a ship's doctor, I referred to Robertson.

But that is not how the original statement reads. Furthermore, "he is like myself, a ship's doctor" implies that both parties are *currently* engaged in a medical capacity, whereas Statham claimed at the outset to have no current occupation.

> I don't say Dr Robertson is of Maine. I think he has gone there. He is an Englishman with British qualifications, so I have always understood. He left England the second day after I took second document to Mr Stokes. It was copied in the press.

What then was this second document, and what was the date of Robertson's letter, which could not have arrived at the very same time the author left Liverpool for the USA unless written beforehand?

On the occasion I saw Mr Stokes he asked me to put it down and bring it round to him.

Put what down? Robertson's statement/confession?

I think the day I went with the half sheets was the third day after.

After what?

I am certain I left the half sheets with Mr Stokes.

Not with his clerk then.

I called the day after. Mr Stokes returned the half sheets he said he had taken a copy of them.

The letter did not remain in my possession.

By Maine I mean Boston in the state of Maine.

I have not a 'lot' of uterine sounds but other instruments pertaining to the uterus.

When it is stated, 'I thought Mr Stokes should have subpoenaed Robertson', I said 'Why don't you – and Mr Stokes replied, 'No we don't want him now. Wait until we go to the Old Bailey.'

I paid more than £4. I find I paid Hansen £4 alone.

Cross examined:

It was the transport 'Clara' I was in not the 'Pearl Corvette'

To what 'Pearl' did the earlier statement refer therefore? It could hardly have been Pearl Harbour!

I was senior midshipman in the Clara.

Considering the officers and crew of the Pearl Corvette served with distinction at the time of the Indian Mutiny as 'Pearl's Naval Brigade', whereas the duties imposed upon the transport Clara were altogether more mundane (e.g., conveying convicts to Western Australia in 1864), the motive for Henry Statham's metaphorically 'jumping ship' becomes apparent.

It was in June 1860 I became Instructor of Musketry.

Because of (or as well as) resigning the Queen's commission as Ensign?

> My employment for Mr Maynard was on two
> occasions only. My pension is not from the
> Queen at all.
>
> (Signed) Henry Statham
>
> (Signed) taken and sworn before me
>
> L.T. d'Eyncourt

The introduction of this witness, Dr Henry Statham, is as questionable as the evidence he provided. What more extreme an instance of 'braggadocio' might one expect to encounter than someone declaring themselves willing to confess to a felony, in relation to which capital punishment was inevitable if convicted, simply in order to exonerate a complete stranger? And 'stranger' is very much the operative word here. The very fact that Statham was subpoenaed as a witness for the defence (court subpoenas in capital cases being a rare occurrence in Victorian jurisprudence) indicates that he was not exactly a willing participant in these proceedings.

The ploy of calling upon an unverifiable third-party to account for a crime is not uncommon. In 2004 a 'whole life' sentence (later reduced to 37 years) was passed on former US Marine, and police killer, David Bieber, who, toward the close of his defence at Newcastle Crown Court, claimed he knew the identity of the assassin, but would have to protect his anonymity for fear of reprisal against either himself or his own family in the USA. Similarly, here we have the tale of a Dr Robertson, casually announcing his complicity in a murder case, apparently, just before taking ship across the Atlantic.

The mere existence of this Dr Robertson, when viewed against the cascade of inaccuracies exhibited in the remainder of Statham's testimony, is questionable to say the least.

Despite various denials of prior acquaintance ('I never saw Mrs Schummacher in my life' and 'I did not know anyone named Gardener' but 'Yes I know *Dr* Gardener') the conclusion seems inescapable that Gloster's defence were looking to yet another of Eliza Schummacher's acquaintances as an explanation for what must have happened to her that Monday afternoon. Correspondence through the equally elusive Miss Brady (now somewhere near Paris, France - arguably a more feminine destination than the USA), was potentially pivotal in that respect. 'Dr' Statham's comments once again:

> I have seen some letters in connection with this case in the possession of Dr Robertson - one or two signed, I think, yours faithfully Mrs Schummacher.

> I told Mr Stokes I could give Robertson's name and address and said I thought he ought to have subpoenaed him. I didn't give his name and address. I never had Mrs Schummacher's letters except a torn one a few hours. The envelope produced addressed to me is written by a Miss Brady.

> I understood and told Mr Stokes that that letter was written by someone who had worked for

> Mrs Schummacher. I have not the letter. I tore
> it up and kept the envelope.

First, Statham admits to having seen letters signed by the victim in the possession of his associate, Robertson. Although he *could have* provided Mr Stokes with Robertson's address, he did not. And yet he thought Stokes ought (already) to have subpoenaed him. How might Stokes have accomplished that *before* being in receipt of the address he was never given? Noticeably, on reading back his statement, the witness conveniently changes the tense covering his remark to Stokes, from 'he ought to have' to 'why don't you?'

Statham goes on to describe having been in possession of a 'torn' example 'a few hours'. Next he refers to an envelope addressed to himself and written by a Miss Brady, who, it transpires, had worked for Mrs Schummacher. Unbelievably, he proceeds to tear up this letter while keeping the envelope!

Untwisting this deliberately tangled logic, it is clearly *this* letter, *since* torn, that Statham had in his possession for a few hours. Addressed to him in the first instance, it was not torn before he acquired it, but afterwards, when *he* tore it up. From which we may infer that Mrs Schummacher and Henry Statham were *directly connected* via correspondence, and that Statham's source of letters from the victim in this case was not entirely second-hand, as he wished to imply.

This was indeed the gist of the questioning put to Fanny Garwood, who was obviously shown the envelope bearing Statham's name as the addressee, and which she personally did not recognise. Speaking on behalf of her sister Eugenie, she deposed that he was a stranger to her also.

With Statham's self-incriminating testimony on the record, Dr Gloster's counsel, Mr Gill, must have thought all his Christmases had come at once. Even the Magistrate, Mr d'Eyncourt, was moved to opine that the witness had told 'a most extraordinary tale', to which Mr Gill responded:

> I do not wish to go into all the reasons that induced me to call this man, but I intimated them to my friend and Mr Safford, the Chief Clerk. He volunteered this evidence and it was thought advisable that there should be some record of what he was prepared to swear.

Mr d'Eyncourt returned with,

> I can only repeat that it is a very strange story indeed.

The case nevertheless proceeded to Crown Court, with Mr Gill asking for, and being granted, bail on behalf of his beleaguered client.

Once the case was scheduled for trial at the Central Criminal Court, Gloster's fate became altogether more uncertain. But what did that decision on the part of Magistrate d'Eyncourt have to say about the credibility of Dr Henry Statham as a witness, and his story of 'the other man'?

To put not too fine a point on it, the evidence offered by Dr Henry Statham, far from being exculpatory, was dismissed. Very little is known of the interaction between this witness and counsel, but he may have been humiliated in court into the bargain. It was, after all, Dr Gloster's attorney, Mr Gill, who questioned him before the Magistrate and repeatedly asked prosecution witnesses whether they had any knowledge of this man. In effect, Dr Henry Statham, having been subpoenaed to attend the court, then had his integrity called into question by one Irishman in defence of another; one whom *he* was supposed to be helping. On top of which his personal crusade, to liberate the 'poor beggar' he deemed unjustly accused, had manifestly failed.

As banal as it may appear, this could perhaps have been a cue for American-style vengeance, against both the 'blight on humanity' walking the streets of Whitechapel at night *and* the English justice system, while at the same time casting a disparaging slur on the Irish.

*It should be noted for future reference that *Clifford's* Inn, once the oldest of the Inns of Chancery, is in Fetter Lane, off Fleet Street, in the London postal district EC4 (adjacent to the City of London). Chancery Lane (High Holborn, WC1) is within easy walking distance.

CHAPTER 11

SUMMING UP

It is now time we salvaged a few probabilities from the deluge of possibilities before us. Some 'cross-tabulation' should help.

Considering the expert opinion of Dr Bond alongside the spontaneous account given to Sergeant Clough by the affable Dr Louis Tarrico, it is highly likely that Eliza Schummacher suffered her fatal injury over the Sunday/Monday $17^{th}/18^{th}$ June. She was perfectly mobile on the 16th according to her sister.

Tarrico's identification of Dr Gloster as accompanying a female 'friend' to see him 8 to 10 (actually 7 to 9) days before his own arrest on the 1st July suggests, rather implausibly, that Dr Gloster was invited to attend *two* lady patient-friends during the month of June, each complaining of the same symptoms. If Tarrico's timing is accurate, Gloster *cannot* then (between the 21st and 23rd June) have visited him in the company of Eliza Schummacher. It *must* have been someone else. But we have heard from at least two sources (Eliza and her sister Emily Maud) that Dr Tarrico had been identified to the patient prior to the 8th June (the date of their joint visit). There was an interval of some nine or ten days therefore during which Eliza could have travelled to Wardour Street once or twice more, either alone or in company. She may have done so earlier than that even.

Among the many peculiarities of the evidence is a wide discrepancy between the various accounts of Eliza Schummacher's first significant interaction with the male midwife from Kensington. At the time of her dying statement, she referred to her visit to Dr Tarrico 'four weeks last Thursday' (May 31st). She called on Dr Gloster 'the next day', which would have been Friday the 1ˢᵗ June – four clear days before Gloster himself claims to have received Mrs Schummacher at his practice, on Tuesday evening, the 5ᵗʰ June (when all other references by the patient are to the 4ᵗʰ, i.e., the Monday).

Eliza described Tarrico as 'passing an instrument' gently, Dr Gloster as doing so painfully, whereas Tarrico recalled examining just the one lady patient, at Dr Gloster's request, and without the use of an instrument at all, having calmed her fears and dismissed her pleas for chloroform. In her dying statement Eliza went on to accuse Dr Gloster of visiting her on the 11ᵗʰ June (when in reality she visited *him*) and yet again 'passing an instrument' in such a way that she had ever since been unable to get up on account of the pain. But staff at her Moreton Place workshop failed to notice anything untoward until a week later, and she herself was at her work when Emily Maud called on the 16ᵗʰ.

All things considered, it appears Dr Tarrico and his prospective patient were each well wide of the mark in their timing of events, albeit for different reasons.

The conclusion that Dr Gloster's visit to 22 Wardour Street took place in the company and interests of Eliza Schummacher is not at all unreasonable. Whether Tarrico actually 'passed an instrument' on that occasion scarcely matters, since the patient herself described him as 'gentle'. The wound that would ultimately despatch her was brutal.

Coming down on the side of collusion between doctor and patient however calls into question the position of ignorance adopted by the practitioner, who on the one hand maintained that he never once suggested the Soho man's name, yet on the other seems to have escorted the patient to him personally. On balance one might further conclude that he simply gave in to her entreaties and took a risk, the result being a combination of bad luck and ineptitude, a collusion more typical of manslaughter than murder.

The fatal blow was most probably struck somewhere other than at the Moreton place home of the deceased. The one thing nobody from the household reported hearing on either the Monday or Tuesday afternoon was an agonized scream from someone whose pain threshold was low enough for them to have elsewhere requested chloroform. Chloroform was not brought to the house in either a Gladstone bag or an apothecary's chest. Neither accessory was seen being carried in or out on the Monday afternoon, nor were traces of anaesthetic detectable after the visiting doctor, whoever it may have been, had left.

Dr Crane's replies under cross-examination, to questions concerning his transcription of the victim's dying statement, appear to support this conclusion:

> On the Friday 22nd I first saw Mrs Schummacher. I took some note of dates. I had that day formed an opinion something serious had happened, and that day Dr Gloster's name was mentioned to me. I was then thoroughly alive to the importance of the matter. Any charge, whether he is guilty or innocent, made against a medical man is a very grave thing – I thought then it was likely the woman would not recover – I thought it was better for everybody that another person should be present – I thought it was best for myself –
>
> I produce the notes I made on an (margin note: put in) old letter. Marked 5 –
>
> I took down 22nd June, written by a stylographic pen.
>
> 'Went to see G last Tuesday three weeks'.

That is when she said. Don't know if that would be the 26th May. – Referring to an almanac I think Tuesday 29th May. –

'and Monday following'. I should say that means 4th June.

'Monday week at his own house Dr G used an instrument on 11th June *and again last Monday.*'

She told me as much as, Dr Gloster performed an operation on her at Dr Gloster's house –

I took no notes except this and the dying declaration.

I can't remember (in answer to question unknown) she said on Monday week at his own house used an instrument, but you must take it so as it is in my note.

I didn't ask her to describe what took place at his house. She did not give the description of what took place at Dr Gloster's house – with the exception of what she told me in the dying declaration which was reduced to writing.

Dr Gloster's own muddled denial of *visits made* is a touch vacuous when assessed together with the significance of *visits received*. But then we have some 'little bottles' downstairs at Moreton Place to take into account.

The only bottle doctor Gloster will have carried in his pocket was the ergot, supplied after Eliza had 'sent for him', on the Tuesday presumably, when he did not 'pass an instrument', although Emily Maud claimed to have seen a bottle of medicine in the house late on the Monday afternoon, which she proceeded to administer to her sister. But was this *the* bottle of most significance? Under cross-examination Emily explained how she 'used to go into her (sister's) bedroom' and 'had sometimes seen bottles of medicine there'.

It is far from certain therefore that Emily was unwittingly administering ergot *from the Monday*. But how, in any case, might Dr Gloster have known to bring that particular medicine with him, whether on the Monday *or* the Tuesday, having not previously attended to the patient's condition himself and with Tuesday morning's telegram saying nothing at all specific, leaving him simply to assume a 'serious illness' of some kind, or so he said?

It was only after her return from 'Lady somebody or other' in Kensington that Monday afternoon, the 18th June, that Eliza Schummacher exhibited signs of distress (no doubt associated with the blood Emily Maud noticed on her sister's chemise around 6.30 p.m. that same evening). The fact that she had been able to visit 'Lady Somebody' at all for much of the day, having left in the morning and returned in the afternoon, according to Mrs Burles, argues against any internal operation having been performed the day before. The Monday walk to her door, following her trip to Kensington, was no doubt the last she undertook.

Having been to Dr Gloster's practice the previous week, returning with a 'billet-doux' as proof of her visit, she knew full well what facilities were on offer. And since Dr Gloster was occasionally reliant on an 'assistant', Eliza's pained reference to what 'they' had done did not necessarily implicate Louis Tarrico.

Taking everything into consideration, a conclusion may be reached on the strength, literally, of the smallest of details – the little bottle of ergot that stood as a silent witness to events.

This is how chemist Thomas Stevenson spoke of the substance when called to give evidence:

Thomas Stevenson sworn.

I am Professor of Chemistry at Guys Hospital and lecturer on Medical Jurisprudence.

On the 18th I received the bottle produced personally from Manley. It contained nearly one dose and was sealed up.

I analysed it.

It is a solution of ergot. It would be composed of 30 or 40 grains of the extract of ergot according to the Pharmacopia per fluid ounce. This is a bottle divided into eight doses; an 8 oz. bottle. Ergot is a proper medicine which may be used by a medical man and is a medicine which being taken internally will act directly on the uterus. Ergot is a scheduled poison of the Poisons Act. If action of the womb was set up by an instrument or in any other way, ergot of rye will cause a continuance of the contractions of the womb and strengthen them so as to cause the expulsion of its contents. I think it is very doubtful whether that quantity of ergot given to a pregnant woman would cause abortion of itself – it would be an improper medicine for a woman to take except under medical advice.

Ergot of rye is more commonly given to restrain excessive menstruation. It is also used at times to bring menses on.

To a woman not pregnant it might if administered for a long period be prejudicial to life but not for a short period.

I am speaking of it in the strength of that produced.

(signed) Thomas Stevenson

It is clear from Stevenson's testimony that ergot, although potentially fatal to an unborn child, has other, more positive medicinal uses. Without assuming any physical intrusion upon Eliza Schummacher's person by Dr Gloster, it is entirely possible that he prescribed the ergot for a purpose other than to encourage expulsion of the contents of her womb. As Stevenson observed, 'I think it is very doubtful whether that quantity of ergot given to a pregnant woman would cause abortion of itself.'

We must of course take into account that no-one was really sure quite what state of conception Eliza Schummacher was in at the time, if any. However, a single word, 'let slip' by Dr Gloster, who was undeniably the gentleman to have visited Eliza Schummacher on Tuesday the 19th June, appears to clarify his motives in this instance.

Recalling his interaction on the Wednesday with the desperate but luckless Emily Maud, we may note from their exchange the following, which the lady witness deposed on the 17th July:

> He said you go back to your sister and tell her
> to send you to Dr Tarrico and say she is in great
> pain, and she had got a show and that he would
> come to her alone and charge her two guineas.

Although it crops up during the testimony of Emily Maud Baker, Dr Gloster's use of the phrase 'got a show' here tells us all we need to know about why, exactly, he would have brought the ergot with him to 21 Moreton Place, whether on the Monday *or* the Tuesday.

As Thomas Stevenson informed the court, ergot, if taken in the dosage represented by the 8 oz. bottle dispensed, would not, of itself, induce termination, although small doses could reasonably be administered with a view to controlling menstruation. Dr Gloster's instruction to Emily Maud however includes unmistakeable reference to the female experience at the onset of labour.

Before contractions commence in earnest, the initial release of a plug of mucus from the mouth of the uterus is described, in medical parlance, as 'a show'. If that is what Dr Gloster took to have happened in the case of his patient Eliza Schummacher, then, clearly, his expectation of the ergot could not have been that of either minimizing or encouraging menstruation. And if the ergot alone were insufficient to do the job, so to speak, then he must also have known that other measures had been employed, and he can only have done that by being a party to them. He could not have introduced *that* medicine 'just in case', and without knowing what had preceded it.

Finally, if it took a telegram on the Tuesday morning for Dr Gloster to appear with any urgency that afternoon, it would have taken a similar note of desperation to procure the services of any other practitioner within just a few hours of a metaphorically abortive visit to Kensington the day before. There are no accounts from any quarter of a 'medical man', competent or otherwise, being notified or placed 'on standby' in the case of Eliza Schummacher. Except, perhaps, for the unknown contents of the letter written by Miss Brady to Dr Henry Statham.

CHAPTER 12

THE VERDICT

Regina vs Gloster was an open and shut case – literally. Crown court proceedings opened at the Old Bailey on Monday the 24th September and closed the next day. Following further submission of the medical evidence on the Tuesday, Mr Poland proposed to enter Eliza Schummacher's dying statement on behalf of the Crown. Gloster's counsel, Mr Gill, challenged this intention, arguing that Eliza Schumacher's was not a *bona fide* 'dying statement' in the eyes of the law, as the author could not be said to have known beyond question she was dying. She did not, it was argued, have a 'settled and hopeless expectation of impending death'. Her statement, suggested as having been made at the invitation of Dr Crane, was therefore inadmissible as evidence for the cause of her undeniable distress. The judge, Mr Justice Charles, decided in favour of the defence.

Finding himself suddenly bereft of crucial eye witness testimony, Mr Poland took the view that he ought not to proceed with the case for the prosecution, the victim's 'dying statement' being the only direct evidence he had to bring before the court. Interestingly, as reported in the Times the day after, Gloster's counsel, Mr Gill, added that he had a mass of evidence to be called, if necessary, on the part of the defence, and he was prepared to show by what appeared to be conclusive evidence, that Mr Gloster was not at the house on June 18th. An interesting observation indeed, since merely being present at 21 Moreton Place on any given date was not at all the substantive issue.

Mr Justice Charles proceeded to address the jury, instructing them that it would be their duty to find the defendant *not guilty*. Accordingly they returned their verdict as directed and the defendant was discharged.

Just as professional boxers are always alert to (and probe for) the possibility of an early exit, Mr Gill's recourse to a 'point of law' is not an inevitable sign of weakness in the defence case. Nonetheless he took full advantage of the position on behalf of his client. Dr James Gloster left the court a free man, all charges against him having been dropped.

That was on the 25th September 1888, five days before the grossly mutilated body of Catherine Eddowes was discovered lying in Mitre Square, Whitechapel, her abdomen torn open by someone at least familiar with anatomy, and who subsequently boasted, in a message chalked on a tenement wall just a few minutes' walk away, that a certain category of individual 'would not be blamed for nothing'.

CHAPTER 13

UNFINISHED BUSINESS

Whoever robbed Catherine Eddowes of her life quite possibly participated in the murder also of Martha Tabram, an East End 'unfortunate', who, like Eliza Schummacher, was thirty-nine years old at the time of her death. Unlike Eliza however she suffered no fewer than *thirty-nine* stab wounds to her torso, whereas Mrs Schummacher endured just the one, inflicted internally.

Martha Tabram was assaulted in the early hours of the 7th August, while Dr James Gloster was being held on remand in Holloway jail. 'Polly' Nichols was found murdered in Buck's Row, Whitechapel, on the 31st August, Annie Chapman behind no. 29 Hanbury Street on the 8th September; dates when Dr James Gloster was in fact at liberty, having met the conditions of his bail in the sum of £450 on August 23rd.

The death of Catherine Eddowes on the 30th September followed immediately upon that of Elizabeth Stride, whose body, left lying in the Berner Street yard of a working men's club (Duffield yard), was not yet cold. Meanwhile Eddowes was about to be quietly 'anatomized' elsewhere.

The last generally accepted victim of the infamous Whitechapel murderer, Mary Jane Kelly's abominated corpse was found inside her own lodgings at 13 Miller's Court on the morning of the 9th November, the day of the Lord Mayor's parade.

With evidence in the Gloster case tending to incriminate rather than exonerate and the unsolicited testimony of maverick doctor Henry Statham serving to confuse rather than clarify, the accused stood in some jeopardy of losing rather more than his livelihood.

Whoever was ultimately responsible for the death, accidentally or otherwise, of Eliza Schummacher, there can be no denying the purposeful assassination of a handful of 'fallen women' in London's East End that autumn. 'Bad' to differing degrees, four of them at least would have 'smelled of spirits' at the time they were slain.

There is a singularly notorious item of correspondence associated with the Whitechapel murders, which has come to be widely known as 'the Lusk letter'. A taunting, grotesquely morbid communication, written to accompany a packaged portion of human kidney (most probably that of Catherine Eddowes) and addressed to George Lusk, a local builder/restorer of theatres and Chairman of the so-called Whitechapel Vigilance Committee, it features several dialectic allusions to Ireland, one in particular to Limerick, birthplace of Dr James Cockburn Gloster, a medical graduate of Dublin University and former student at the London Hospital, Whitechapel.

Another letter of some relevance to the Whitechapel crimes (dated the 19th October and addressed to one Dr Forbes Winslow) mentions a name which, although visually ambiguous within the original, has an Italian 'ring' to it, ending in the letters 'igi'. The anonymous author correctly predicts the date of the final East End outrage, but errs in suggesting it might occur in either the West End or Clapham.

Dr Gloster, we know, had an Italian-speaking associate in the West End, while his sometime 'assistant', Dr Meredith Townsend, had earlier (1869) shared an address in Clapham (Thurlow House, Clapham Rise), probably with his father (Henry Meredith Townsend, LSA, who later (1888) lived at no. 328 Clapham Road).

Written at the head of this same letter, by the author as like as not, was the address, '22 Hammersmith Road, Chelsea'.

Hammersmith Road forms a continuation of Kensington High Street and was clearly identified as such within the London Post Office Directories of the period. Number 22 was occupied in the 1880s by one Charles Robert Tennant, a Dubliner by birth. The exact location of this address is just along from Upper Phillimore Place (Kensington High Street), where Dr James Gloster had his practice.

Yet another letter recorded in the archives and signed 'Jack the Ripper' was actually found lying in Victoria Road, not fifteen minutes' walk away.

Can all of this really be mere coincidence, or was the bombast of Henry Statham, allied to the indignation of Dr James Gloster, taken to brutal extremes, on the supposition that 'the poor beggar' (Gloster) might not have escaped the noose, or that 'Dr' Henry Statham might afterwards have been obliged to step into the limelight himself?

The supposition of even a tenuous connection between a botched operation performed on a 'dressmaker' from Pimlico and the bestial slaughter of half-a-dozen prostitutes in London's East End will no doubt appear to some as the by-product of an overly fertile imagination, suggesting as it does a stark migration of purpose, from the unsanitary in one quarter to the downright sordid in another. However, as a very dear friend of mine once said when describing the pursuit of archaeology, 'Context is everything.' And context, in the case of Regina vs. Gloster, was something about which almost the entire cast of the drama were in denial; all except the defence counsel, Mr Charles Gill, who, in lifting the curtain at the edges, took care not to expose the exact position of his client standing centre-stage.

In a learned article published more than twenty-five years previously (1862), social researcher Henry Mayhew provided *exactly* the detail required for us to understand what really transpired between Dr James Gloster and Eliza Schummacher during the month of June, 1888. In the course of his thorough-going discussion of certain clandestine business practices, Mayhew considers the role of the procuress:

> The procuresses who keep introducing houses often take in women to lodge and board. But they are quite independent, and must be well known about town, and kept by someone, or the procuress, if she is, comparatively speaking, in any position, will not receive them.
>
> To show how the matter is accomplished let us suppose an introducing house of notoriety and good report in its way, somewhere in the neighbourhood of St. George's Road, Pimlico, a district which, I may observe, is prolific in loose women.

Ironically, 44 St George Road, Pimlico was later home to Metropolitan Police Commissioner, Sir Charles Warren. It is this very thoroughfare, identified within London street maps of today as St George's *Drive,* to which Mayhew is referring. We know that to be the case, as he later mentions:

> Stanley Street, or Winchester Street, which streets everybody knows are contiguous to St. George's Road, and inhabited by beauty that ridicules decorum and laughs at the virtuous restrictions that are highly conducive to a state of single blessedness and a condition of old-maidism.

Winchester Street remains to this day contiguous (to use Mayhew's phrase) with St George's *Drive.* The Moreton Triangle, as it is nowadays referred to, is literally 'just down the road'.

Hence we have thirty-nine-year-old Eliza Schummacher, four or five years separated from her husband, who has spent the past seven years in Moreton Place, albeit at four different addresses, thereby consolidating her presence in an area by now well known for its being 'prolific in loose women'. She too keeps female lodgers and is frequently out of the house herself.

Unfortunately Eliza did not survive to be numbered among the population at the time of the 1891 census. However, ten years earlier she is known to have been living with a one-year-old son in Charlwood Street (which traverses St George's Drive and connects directly with Moreton Place), though not as Mrs Schummacher. Her 1881 census record is that of Eliza Jane Baker (Emily Maud Baker of course being her sister). Sadly her little boy died the following year.

The ensuing eighteen months must have been eventful in the extreme for Eliza, with marriage to a gentleman's servant (surname Schummacher), another male child, and re-location to Moreton place. But of *Mr* Schummacher there is no trace. Even in 1891 there were more Schummachers resident in Ireland than in England, and neither of the *only two* to appear within the mainland census record at that time can have had any connection to Eliza Jane of Pimlico.

Nor has it been possible to confirm that Eliza's second son was genuinely a Schummacher, any more than one can be at all certain about the four or five 'miscarriages' she may have suffered since (although how Mr Charles Gill came by *that* piece of information and Eliza's sisters not so is an interesting question in itself. Perhaps his client, Dr Gloster, was in a position to flout doctor-patient privilege to personal advantage. Perhaps the miscarriages in question were induced. Who knows?). When all is said and done, no lady tailoress ever got pregnant as a result of dropping a stitch.

Would another unwanted pregnancy really have interfered with Eliza's *dressmaking* career therefore?

Respectably married, even if only in name, Eliza is thus continuously resident at the heart, almost, of an up-market 'red light' district, from which base of operations (no pun intended) she makes the acquaintance of an affluent male doctor from nearby South Kensington, whom she knows for almost as long as she is separated from her husband, and who appears to have been rather cavalier toward her with at least five pounds of his own money. At this point we should turn again to Mayhew's detailed exposition, and his account of the choreography of negotiation, so to speak:

> A well-known professional man, a wealthy merchant, an M.P., or a rich landed proprietor, calls upon the lady of the house, orders some champagne, and enters into conversation about indifferent matters, until he is able delicately to broach the object he has in view. He explains that he wishes to meet with a quiet lady whose secrecy he can rely upon, and whom he can trust in every possible way. He would like her, we will imagine, to be vivacious, witty, and gay.
>
> The lady of the house listens complacently, and replies that she knows someone who exactly answers the description the amorous M.P. has given, and says that *she will send a message to her at once if he wishes*, but he must take his chance of her being at home; if she is out, an appointment will be made for the next day. In the meantime a messenger is despatched to the lady in question, who in all probability does not reside at any great

distance.....Some more champagne is ordered
and consumed, every bottle of which costs the
consumer fifteen shillings, making a profit to
the vendor of at least seventy per cent. When
the lady arrives, the introduction takes place,
and the matter is finally arranged as far as the
introducer is concerned. The woman so
introduced generally gives half the money she
obtains from the man to the keeper of the
house for the introduction.

For 'champagne' here read 'gin'. Remember also 'Come at
once, Moreton' and the ensuing argument said telegram caused
between Dr Gloster and the unwitting Emily Maud, how 'his
name was his name', and how he 'would not be seen in the
neighbourhood again were she to lay down £500 that minute'.
Not forgetting, of course, the tell-tale question the doctor, having
relented, put to Mrs Burles at the close of his ultimate visit: 'You
have never seen me before have you?'

In an act of pre-cognition almost, Henry Mayhew has described
precisely what a local telegrapher is very likely to have construed
from the urgent despatch authored by Mrs Burles on Eliza
Schummacher's behalf, and why Dr Gloster, with a reputation to
protect, was so incensed at the publication of his name in the
context of his being summoned to an unspecified address at
Moreton Place.

In short, Eliza Schummacher (née Baker) was rather more
than a dressmaker struggling to make ends meet. She ran a parallel
business concerned with making entirely different ends meet. Dr
James Gloster knew of her alternative source of income and was
perhaps among her clientele, as may have been Mr Gilbert and
the other men who took just a few steps to pass in front of the

downstairs window, but without necessarily attracting the attention of Mary Hull.

Regina vs. Gloster therefore was not solely, or at all, a matter of medical incompetence perpetrated upon a naïve, sober, and unsuspecting female. Eliza Schummacher was, as Dr Gloster was prepared to disclose to the police who arrested him, a 'bad', and no doubt, on occasion, 'drunken' woman - not an assessment he can have made on the basis of attending her young son several years past, nor his more recent attempts to dissuade the importunate lady from seeking an abortion.

And so we proceed to Whitechapel, where, thanks to law enforcement directives by none other than Pimlico resident Sir Charles Warren, instructions which effectively relaxed police control of the 'oldest profession', a handful of brazen, inebriate prostitutes, whose status was considerably beneath that of the short-term brides of Belgravia, would become tokens of vengeance against their kind.

CHAPTER 14

THAT 'CUT ABOVE'

With the true nature of the Schummacher episode revealed, a connection between it and the Whitechapel murders which followed becomes plausible. Besides the accused, Dr James Cockburn Gloster ('My name is my name'), another medical man of dubious accomplishment had his own grounds for indignation, having been subpoenaed to attend as a witness for the defence, then repeatedly referred to by counsel - as an alternative suspect almost. Dismissing any notion that the identities of the Whitechapel victims were in any way significant in themselves, we are left with a handful of homicides, the interpretation of which may draw informatively upon this prior context.

The extent, or absence, of Jack the Ripper's surgical skill has been a bone of contention since the Whitechapel atrocities were committed. The view of surgical practitioners nowadays, however, is that the anatomical abuse of his victims, in the manner conducted and in the time available, would not have been possible had he been working from a position of ignorance. Whereas a butcher might have shared the necessary degree of expertise, just, those involved in the up-market backdrop to these downtown crimes were qualified surgeons, apparently, embroiled in issues of abortion and all that that entails. Furthermore, there are grounds for considering the possibility that the post-mortem injuries inflicted upon the ripper's earlier victims were not evidence of random assault at all, but had a genuine medico-legal connotation.

On the 5th May 1760, Laurence Shirley, the 4th Earl Ferrers, was hanged at Tyburn for the murder of his family steward, John Johnson. It is not the detail of his crime which is of interest, but what was done with his body after death. Ferrers' corpse was transported to the city, where it was dissected. The Newgate Calendar describes the proceedings thus:

> The accustomed time of one hour being past, the coffin was raised up, with the greatest decency, to receive the body; and, being deposited in the hearse, was conveyed by the sheriffs, with the same procession, to Surgeons' Hall, to undergo the remainder of the sentence. A large incision was then made from the neck to the bottom of the breast, and another across the throat; the lower part of the belly was laid open, and the bowels taken away. It was afterwards publicly exposed to view in a room up one pair of stairs at the Hall; and on the evening of Thursday, the 8th of May, it was delivered to his friends for interment.

This practice of 'anatomization', as performed in late 18th c. England, persisted well into the reign of Queen Victoria, when the thirst for whatever knowledge it conferred outstripped the supply of criminal corpses upon which it might be exercised. Deaths among the workhouse poor soon made up the shortfall in that regard. That aside, it is startling to read what is, in effect, a rather precise description of surgical routines practised on the streets of London's Whitechapel a century and more after the treatment meted out to Earl Ferrers.

The hypothesis that the Whitechapel murderer's victims were punished as representatives of their kind, namely 'bad drunken women', would appear to have some merit. However, should there prove to have been an executive connection between the fate of Eliza Schummacher, her dying accusation, and the subsequent

Whitechapel crimes, which of the protagonists so far identified might have been directly involved in both escapades, and why?

Dr Gloster should have been in fear of his life come September 1888, there being no such thing as a court of appeal as far as Victorian jurisprudence was concerned. Dr Henry Statham was not in the same position exactly, although Gloster's counsel may well have been keen on putting him there; as was Statham to volunteer for the role, having announced his suicidal readiness to confess to the crime 'if it would get the poor beggar (Gloster) off'.

Indignation was a sentiment clearly expressed within the Goulston Street graffito, hence someone in Dr James Gloster's position that autumn might conceivably have adopted the attitude of one who would rather 'not be blamed for nothing'. Thanks to the skill of his legal representatives, as well as his own financial resources, he was actually at liberty when the (canonical five) Whitechapel murders were committed, despite being accused of homicide himself.

Further pointers come in the form of hints, here and there, of Irish involvement in the Whitechapel crimes. Sir Charles Warren's seemingly random opinion notwithstanding, young Emily Marsh, minding her father's leather goods shop in Jubilee Street, was asked for the address of George Lusk by a man thought to have had an Irish accent, whilst the 'Letter from hell' Lusk received subsequently, contained additional linguistic markers; specifically, an instance of Limerick dialect, hinted at in the sign-off ('Mishter Lusk'). Like Mary Jane Kelly, James Gloster was a child of Limerick.

If one's focus were on 'means, motive and opportunity', then Dr James Gloster may be said to have embodied all three. Extraordinarily, and despite the charge laid against him, Dr Gloster was actually at liberty, on bail, prior to the end of August, and fully discharged by the end of September. There are, however, good grounds for not coming immediately to the obvious conclusion. Speaking with an Irish accent does not, in and of itself, confer nationality; nor does the writing of dialectic inflections, these being *spoken* attributes which do not typically impinge upon an author's literacy. Someone intent on identifying the Irish (as opposed to identifying *with* them), is just as reasonable a proposition. Now who might have wished to do that?

Dr Henry Statham was unduly keen, for whatever reason, to involve himself in the Schummacher case in defence of the accused Dr Gloster, whom he did not know from Adam. Gloster turned out to be an Irishman, so too his defence counsel, although Statham would not have realised that until being subpoenaed by him to appear in court and immediately put up as a 'straw man'; behaviour far more likely to elicit animosity than be seen as a show of gratitude.

Henry George Algernon Sydney Statham was a man with American friends, American sympathies, and quite possibly considered himself to be a naturalised American, having lived and studied in the USA for a number of years. This was in an age of almost unlimited freedom of movement among populations, before the advent of international passports. Indeed press reports at the time described Statham as 'American'. Intriguingly, and with an open field when it came to potential suspects for the Whitechapel murders, the Metropolitan Police demonstrated a peculiar interest in Americans.

Inspector John George Littlechild identified the 'quack' American doctor Tumblety as 'a likely one,' a suspicion no doubt fostered by the rumour which surfaced during the inquest into the death of Annie Chapman, that an American doctor had solicited the purchase of female uteri from a London medical school. (Tumblety was said to have been in possession of a collection of such organs.) Surprisingly this rumour was even articulated by the presiding coroner, Wynne Baxter.

Although vigorously refuted by the medical profession at the time (in both the Lancet and the BMJ), the story was picked up by the Chicago Tribune, where it was claimed the doctor in question hailed from Philadelphia, Pennsylvania.

A police report on the investigation's progress mentioned three cowboys, who had arrived the year before (1887) with Buffalo Bill's 'Wild West Show'. That particular spectacle formed part of the American Exhibition at Earl's Court, Kensington - a special feature of Queen Victoria's jubilee celebrations. Having remained behind after the touring company returned to the USA, all three cowboys were traced and 'satisfactorily accounted for themselves', although quite how that was accomplished is a mystery in itself.

The equation of *three* stray cowboys with occasional witness reports of strangers wearing frock-coats and wide-awake hats is somewhat less than obvious. That said, certain items of dress were considered high-fashion items in the American West. They included the 'billycock' hat. Exactly two such accoutrements, a red silk handkerchief and a horseshoe tie-pin, were identified by George Hutchinson as having been worn by the last individual known to have consorted with Mary Jane Kelly. Perhaps the equation was of a different sort however. William 'Buffalo Bill' Cody was a Freemason, as were many other westerners and no doubt some members of his entourage; a prospect which suggests a reason other than fashion sense lay behind the Met's interest in these and other Americans.

The reputedly homosexual Tumblety, standing over six feet tall, was, in reality, more of an *unlikely* one, being among a range of subjects eye-witnesses put at somewhere between 5'3" and 5'10". That did not prevent police from 'tailing' someone, thought to have been Tumblety but travelling by the name of Townsend, all the way across the Atlantic. (Townsend being the surname also of Dr Gloster's neighbourly assistant.)

Did Sir Charles Warren notice something 'American' at Goulston Street, his own 'Irish' interpretation notwithstanding? Or did a suggestive pattern emerge with the demise of Elizabeth Stride and Catherine Eddowes, both on the night of 30th September? Two aspects of the 'double event' suggest just such a possibility.

The barbaric treatment of Catherine Eddowes at Mitre Square, in the City of London, barely an hour after the discovery of Liz Stride's body in Berner Street (within the jurisdiction of the Metropolitan Police), points to the importance, as far as their killer was concerned, of post-mortem mutilation. It also confers particular significance upon the date of commission. Otherwise why should the culprit have persisted that night, knowing the heat would already be on once he had been interrupted elsewhere?

What, therefore, might one read into the *sequence* of dates: 31st, 8th, 30th? Not as much as the Metropolitan Police could perhaps have accomplished once George Lusk was in receipt of his own Gory communication, postmarked 15th October, and which spoke of more to come in 'a whil' (*sic*).

With the month of October already nearing its end, the 9th November might at least have suggested itself to an observant analyst, the more so perhaps had they paid attention to a popular speculation at the time, that the culprit was a traveller of some kind, who could only indulge in murder at the weekend. They might then have noticed, even as early as the date of the double-event, how October 9th fell on a weekday. Completion of the paradigm $31 + 8$, $30 + 9$ would necessarily have to wait until November.

Such foresight may also have influenced the Met's decision to scale back their inquiries dramatically following the slaughter of Mary Jane Kelly, all police aid to the East End being stood down by Christmas. Furthermore, it was the view of Assistant Chief Constable and head of CID, Sir Melville Macnaghten, expressed some six years later (1894), that the Whitechapel murderer had 'five victims and five victims only', despite murderous crime persisting in the East End of London thereafter.

There is a school of thought that the Whitechapel murderer's identity was eventually known to certain echelons of the police and that the investigation was wound down simply because they could not prove their case. Equally reasonable, however, is the hypothesis that investigators knew it was all over, despite their *not* knowing who was responsible. Which begs the question: is it possible the number 39 was of particular significance in this case?

*

Whether one places any personal faith in numerology or the occult, it is important to appreciate that Victorian society was by no means immune to such distractions. There was Freemasonry of course, but the age accommodated other secret societies besides. The Order of the Golden Dawn, for example, had a substantial membership, which included one Oscar Wilde. The possibility of Jack the Ripper's attempting to communicate in a cryptic fashion ought at least to be entertained therefore.

Eye witnesses reported seeing individuals accompanying Stride, Eddowes and Mary Jane Kelly close to their times of death, yet none were described as 'down and out', 'shabby genteel' being the most impoverished interpretation. A police study of reports from officers patrolling Whitechapel inferred that the culprit was 'not among the ordinary denizens of that place'. Hence membership of some fraternity or other cannot be ruled out on the grounds of social class.

Ever since its introduction by Stephen Knight, the hypothesis of Freemasonry's being in some way implicated in the Whitechapel murders has managed to resist total rejection, although debate is often brought to a prompt close with dismissal of the word 'Juwes', coupled with the observation that the ritualistic feature to which it might relate was discarded from the workings of Freemasonry in England a century and more before the Whitechapel murders were committed. As previously noted, however, this particular aspect of Masonic working was retained in the USA, its three principal characters being identified, not as Juwes, but as the 'Ruffians' or 'three hanged men'.

Masonic adherents in the USA typically pursue one of two alternative routes of progression, known as the Scottish Rite and York Rite respectively. The one incorporates thirty steps by which any member may ascend within the hierarchy of the brotherhood, the other ten. However, since both progressions culminate in the same 'degree', it could be argued that the two orders represent a combined total of thirty-nine steps. (Curiously, the old Wembley Stadium incorporated thirty-nine steps leading up to the Royal Box, whilst the venue was often affectionately identified by its 'Twin Towers' – another Masonic reference. 39 steps are also housed within the 19th c. obelisk atop Stoodley Pike in Calderdale, Yorkshire.)

There are further aspects, of American Freemasonry in particular, American life in general, which reflect this same number.

1888 marked the centenary of George Washington's election to the position of Worshipful Master of Alexandria lodge no. 39, whilst thirty-nine delegates, thirteen of them Freemasons, put their signatures to the original United States constitution, in Philadelphia, Pennsylvania. Perhaps most surprising, if not a little eerie, is the origin of the 'flag that never was'.

Twice in American history, citizens, representatives, and flag manufacturers looked forward to the accession of new states that would bring total membership of the Union to thirty-nine. Flags bearing thirty-nine stars were first patented and produced in 1875 with 1876 in view, and Colorado identified as the 'centennial state', a mission fulfilled in August that year. Since the Dakota Territory was also expected to join the union at this time, 39-star flags were produced. In the event, however, Dakota was *not* admitted on this occasion.

A second attempt seemed in prospect a dozen years later when 39-star flags were once again in vogue. By now though the Dakotas were divided in two (north and south) and would be admitted separately, thereby skirting the number 39 altogether.

It is not so much the absence of a thirty-ninth state of the Union which is of interest here as the circumstantial timing of each non-event. Dr Henry Statham left America for England in 1875. The Whitechapel murders were committed in 1888; both periods when the admission of a 39th state will have been widely anticipated.

Having gained his medical and surgical qualifications from the 'University of Pennsylvania', it is entirely possible that Henry Statham was at least aware of the existence of a very particular Masonic apron. Formerly the property of Bro. George Washington, it had been presented to the Grand Lodge of Pennsylvania by the Washington Benevolent Society, on July 3rd, 1829. The Lafayette apron, as it was known, had previously been presented to Washington by his ally, the Marquis de Lafayette, in 1784.

Washington's own memoires extend to thirty-nine volumes. Whether associated with the order or not, no reasonably well-connected resident of Philadelphia could fail to notice the Masonic Temple there; an imposing architectural melange of neo-gothic and byzantine styles. (The name of Dr James Gloster does not in fact appear on the register of members kept by the Grand Lodge in London, whilst his brother Thomas did not join the order until 1893. The fraternal status of Dr Henry Statham is, as yet, unknown.)

As far as 1888 and events in London are concerned however, Eliza Schummacher's being aged thirty-nine at the time of her demise appears to be coincidental. So too the age of thirty-nine-year-old Martha Tabram, who was found stabbed to death on a staircase landing inside George Yard Buildings early on the morning of August 7th. That she was stabbed a total of thirty-nine times is rather less straightforwardly explained away.

During a BBC TV programme first broadcast on the 4th April, 2019 (Jack the Ripper – the case re-opened) eleven murders, all committed in London between 1888 and 1891, were subjected to a HOLMES (Home Office Large Major Enquiry System) analysis. The result strongly suggested the killing of Martha Tabram be considered the first of Jack the Ripper's bloody crimes. Co-presenter and Professor of Criminology, David Wilson went so far as to announce:

> I've got absolutely no doubt that Martha Tabram
> was the first of Jack the Ripper's victims.

Professor Wilson's conclusion has a two-fold implication, the second aspect of which we shall address shortly. For now though, if Martha Tabram's murder did indeed signal the onset of Jack the Ripper's rampage, then Dr James Gloster could not have been responsible for it, as he was being held on remand in Holloway Gaol at the time.

Reminiscent of those algebraic equations where the solution is enabled by expansion, addition of the Tabram case to the Whitechapel canon does more than merely increase the total number of victims, from five to six. It permits a very different interpretation of events to that suggested by the behaviour typical of latter-day serial killers.

Given the culprit's readiness to leave written clues at least, coupled with the possibility that his post-mortem antics were in some way indices of his personal background, one may reasonably wonder what aspect of the Tabram murder, apart from the date, might have been particularly symbolic. The absence of any gross mutilation of the type he inflicted subsequently obliges us to take account of the *number* of wounds in this instance.

As bizarre as it may seem, there exists the possibility that the perpetrator of *all six* murders had in mind to make specific reference to the number 39, a statement first made at the expense of Martha Tabram, then *twice* re-iterated between the 31st August and the 9th November 1888. It is possible also that Sir Charles Warren realised this and/or another peculiarity (e.g., the word 'Juwes' possibly being indicative of *American* Freemasonry), on the night of the double event. The numerical aspect at least would obviously have been more immediately apparent to police, medical examiners, the press and the public had the culprit persisted in simply stabbing his victims to death thirty-nine times. Drawing the symbolism out as he did clearly required greater risk and more victims, but these were in plentiful supply.

When all is said and done there is one very specific connotation senior Freemason Sir Charles Warren would undoubtedly have been alive to. Freemasons the world over are governed by a set of general regulations first adopted by the order in 1721, and of which there are thirty-nine.

Stephen Knight too entertained the idea of the number 39 being of significance in the Whitechapel case, when he wrote:

> There was even significance in the thirty-nine
> days that were allowed to elapse between the
> murder of Eddowes and that of Kelly.

Whatever other coincidences may be identified (e.g., Mary Kelly's address, 13 Miller's court being situated at 26 Dorset Street), there can be no disputing the fact that the number of wounds inflicted upon poor Martha Tabram, and the subsequent dates of the Whitechapel murderer's even more notorious crimes, were under his/her/their control. Both aspects were conceivably the result of deliberate choices therefore.

This interpretation is further suggested by the curious encounter between Emily Marsh and a tall dark stranger, who, having seen a 'reward' poster in the window, called in at her father's shop to inquire after the home address of George Lusk.

That incident occurred at around 1.00 p.m. on the 15th October, the day before Lusk received his gory package. If the stranger in question were to have been the Whitechapel culprit, it would follow that he was in a position to meander around the district on dates of his own choosing, and that the 30th September, fully three weeks after Annie Chapman's murder in Hanbury Street, was itself a deliberately chosen interval, not one imposed by circumstance, such as being aboard a ship somewhere in the meantime. By extrapolation one might reasonably conclude that *all* of the dates were somehow of significance.

A note of caution should however be affixed to any interpretation of events that might hinge upon the Emily Marsh story.

The Whitechapel murderer's enmity toward George Lusk may well have been on account of the latter's petitioning HM government to offer a reward for the killer's capture. That being so, the culprit could only have known of Lusk's recommendations, made on behalf of the Whitechapel Vigilance Committee, by being personally close to the committee's affairs, or by reading Lusk's correspondence with under-secretary of state Godfrey Lushington, as reported in the Times, for instance.

The problem this represents is that Lusk's correspondence was reported verbatim and included his *full* postal address. Had the killer read this for himself, he should have had no need of confirmation from Emily Marsh. Furthermore, Lusk had previously described to the press a strange encounter of his own with an individual fitting the description of Emily Marsh's interlocutor. That took place in a bar lounge on Thursday afternoon, the 4th October, and was preceded by the bearded man's calling first at Lusk's home address, which leads one to the obvious conclusion that he already knew what it was.

CHAPTER 15

SOME FORENSIC LINGUISTICS

It was on the 16th October that George Lusk, local builder, restorer of theatres, and chairman of the Whitechapel Vigilance Committee, received his small parcel, containing a substantial piece of human kidney with a section of renal artery attached, all accompanied by a macabre covering note. Unpunctuated, the note read:

> From hell
>
> Mr Lusk
>
> Sir
>
> I send you half the kidne I took from one woman prasarved it for you tother piece I fried and ate it was very nise I may send you the bloody knif that took it out if you only wate a whil longer.
>
> Signed
>
> Catch me when you can Mishter Lusk

It is a missive which says rather little, yet tells us a good deal.

According to one handwriting expert at least (American, Michelle Dresbold), words like 'Mishter', 'prasarved' and 'tother' are particularly informative. 'Tother' was an Irish contraction, apparently, and 'prasarved' was "the way an Irish speaker would *phonetically* spell it." Dresbold takes this to indicate that "the writer had an Irish background."

Suddenly Dr Gloster has the look of a culprit once more. But how is one to reconcile a Dublin medical school graduate with the dubious level of literacy on display here, where silent letters in word-final position are missing (kidne, knif and whil), the word 'wate' is a phonic imitation of the 'ate' that precedes it, and there are misspelt sibilants ('nise' and 'Mishter')? Might the lack of linguistic sophistication be more apparent than real?

Before addressing that question we need first to establish why the sender should have targeted George Lusk at all, when the bulk of speculative or malicious correspondence in this case was sent either to the Metropolitan Police directly or to the Central News Agency. And, having settled upon George Lusk as their correspondent, how did they know *where* to send the parcel?

As previously noted, a witness (local shopkeeper's daughter Emily Marsh) was apparently asked by a suspicious individual with an Irish accent, if she could read out the address of George Lusk as it appeared in a newspaper of the day. The man is said to have written down what was read to him – Alder*ney* Street, Globe Road. He did not ask for anything to be spelled out. Yet the writer of the letter which arrived with Lusk barely 24 hours later could not, it seems, similarly conclude the word 'kid*ney*' correctly. And what, in any case, was the immediate context within which the name of George Lusk suddenly featured in the press (in both the Times and the Telegraph, each with an obviously literate readership)?

Lusk had written publicly to the Home office with 'advice' and suggestions concerning the possibility of a reward being offered for information leading to the capture of the Whitechapel murderer. The Home Office reply came from under-secretary of state Sir Godfrey Lushington, and was published in the Times of October 15th. Lusk received his more sanguine communique the day following.

The letter 'from hell', signed 'Catch me when you can', was a taunt therefore, from someone very possibly familiar with the newspapers;

someone whose 'word-final' oversights were not mirrored by either word-initial or -medial errors involving 'silent' letters ('<u>k</u>nif' and 'w<u>h</u>il' were each correctly spelt as far as they went, so too the word 'signed' at the close) and whose representation of sibilants was not uniformly in error either ('nise' vs. 'piece').

Nor did phonetic divergence lead to the writing of 'fryed', despite the words 'fried' and 'piece' being *orthographically* alike as regards their vocalic aspect, but phonetically distinct from each other nonetheless. As to the Irish allusions dispersed throughout, the word 'Mishter' hints at the dialect of Limerick (Dr Gloster's home county). It represents what a native of Limerick might *say.* It is not, however, what a literate native of Limerick would *write.*

Perhaps then, the Lusk letter, so called, was written with reference *to* Dr James Gloster, not *by* him. Furthermore, the question of where among persons of Dr Gloster's acquaintance one might look for authorship of this letter can be answered fairly directly, with reference to the testimony of that most eccentric of defence witnesses to give evidence at his trial.

In common with the Goulston Street graffito, the Lusk letter does not give the analytical reader an awful lot to go on, yet the fallacy of semi-literacy and the significance of a third-party reference to Limerick can still be sifted out. Might it have yet more to reveal?

The 'letter' divides neatly into two component parts, the second of which is a coherent and complete sentence ("I may send you the bloody knif that took it out if you only wate a whil longer"). The contour of this sentence, its prosody if you will, is similar to that of a remark made in court by 'Dr' Henry Statham. ("I'd be prepared to say I did it myself if it would get the poor beggar off.")

The first of the letter's two 'paragraphs' ("I send you half the kidne I took from one woman prasarved it for you tother piece I fried and ate it was very nise") holds further surprises. The position within the sentence of 'prasarved it for you', for instance, reflects a similar construct to be found in Dr Statham's witness testimony, where the phrase 'the full of it' also occurs in parenthesis:

All the information, the full of it, is Robertson's.

The letter's very opening comprises a handful of unpunctuated clauses, two of which (3, 4 following) are of particular interest:

1. I send you half the kidne

2. I took from one woman

3. Prasarved it for you

4. Tother piece I fried and ate

5. It was very nise

The word 'woman' in the original *appears* to have been written in the plural, indicating omission of the phrase 'of the' if so. Conversely it might simply be a case of poor handwriting. Read as a stand-alone remark however, the subsequent clause omits the subject (understood) or, if the intention were to relate directly to the subject of the previous statement, a conjunction allowing it to do so (e.g., '*and* preserved for you'). The next clause positions object before subject.

Whilst a similar tendency toward word omission is to be found within the lengthy, rambling statements given in evidence by Dr Henry Statham at the trial of Dr James Gloster (e.g., "I have not any occupation" and "I have not the letter"), rather more startling are instances of structural inversion within the sentence (grammatical structure that is) with object preceding subject, indirect object preceding direct object, etc.

Similar to precedence within the Lusk letter of the phrase, 'tother piece' (forming the clause, 'tother piece I fried and ate'), the following are examples, again taken from Statham's protracted statement, of a penchant for grammatical inversion, such as, "I have not in this matter been asking". Particularly germane is a specific instance of word-order reversal that clearly deviates from conventional 'subject-verb-object' usage, and which virtually echoes the 'tother piece' clause.

> He is like myself a ship's doctor.

> I afterwards called again.

> *The original letter I never had.*

> I didn't mention to him this case.

The Lusk letter is seemingly imbued with stylistic elements reminiscent of Dr Henry Statham's use of English and might therefore be viewed as representative of *his* personal 'idiolect'.

There remains one other comparison to take on board; not with the Lusk letter this time, but the identity of the last person seen in the company of young Mary Jane Kelly (probably the Whitechapel murderer's last victim) in the early hours of the 9th November, 1888. A well-dressed individual ('certain it is that he is not among the usual denizens of this place') was overheard by the inquisitive George Hutchinson to say: "You'll be alright for what I've told you."

It would be quite astonishing if one were to find an exact cognate of this statement among those made by Dr Statham, and indeed we do not. However, he twice makes a remark with similar, secretive overtones:

> ...there were certain instruments I could put him on the way of.

And

> ...there were certain instruments I could put him on the way of finding.

142

A plausible case may thus be made for linguistics introducing us to the real culprit behind the Whitechapel murders, in the shape of an unstable individual, who, in July 1888, was humiliated at Ebury Bridge magistrate's court by the Irish counsel for an Irish defendant, whom he had been subpoenaed to assist in his defence against a charge of murder. The victim, portrayed by her immediate family as upstanding, was conversely described by the accused as having been a 'bad drunken woman'. She was importuning abortion, behaved like a procuress and may even have kept a brothel. We know also, from evidence considered during the course of 'Regina vs. Gloster', that someone currently or formerly a member of the Schummacher household (the recently travelled Miss Brady) had corresponded with Dr Henry Statham, possibly on Mrs Schummacher's behalf. The defence counsel even insinuated that this man knew someone had procured abortion and that the patient herself 'knew how to do it'. The ingredients appear to be largely there.

CHAPTER 16

RITES OF PASSAGE

Based largely on the known behaviour of serial killers during the 20th century, criminologists are wont now to categorize such offenders as either 'marauders', who fan out from their place of residence over time to commit their crimes at a comfortable, almost uniform distance from their home, or 'commuters', who persistently travel from their domicile to their 'killing ground'. This very distinction was adopted by geo-profiler Dr Sam Lundrigan, when interviewed by Emilia Fox and David Wilson for the BBC. On the grounds that over 80% of serial killers studied are seen to have been 'marauders', she proceeded to elucidate the area of Whitechapel in which the murderer probably lived, from which information the co-presenters eventually identified local resident Aaron Kosminski as their culprit.

This binary approach is open to criticism however. It begins with the assumption that the Whitechapel murderer was a serial killer as commonly understood, i.e., with an underlying sexual fetish of some kind, and further conjectures that his behaviour would therefore have been consistent with that of the majority of the sample later categorized as 'marauders'. It fails to take into account the very real possibility that the Whitechapel murderer may well have been a transient lodger in the district. Not so much a marauder as a *commuting* marauder.

The idea of a lodger was indeed postulated at the time and has been the focus of different studies since. It has merit in so far as all of the murders were committed at weekends, which long ago spawned the hypothesis that the guilty party was a traveller of some kind, a seaman perhaps. One ought therefore not to overlook the possibility that the gentleman in question *did* travel to be near the scene of his crimes, but from a neighbouring district as opposed to a distant country.

Looking at a place map of the Whitechapel murders and tabulating the locations of *all six* (including that of Martha Tabram), together with the approximate times of death, suggests Jack the Ripper adopted an orbital route, clockwise from the Whitechapel Road and bounded by Aldgate/Goulston Street - Dorset Street - Hanbury Street - Buck's Row, departing the area just east of the London Hospital following the Nichols and Chapman murders.

Time and location are key factors in appreciating the Whitechapel murderer's movements about London's East End in the autumn of 1888. The essential data, specifically the approximate times of death, are as follows:

1. Martha Tabram, 7th August - George Yard buildings (Gunthorpe Street). Alive at 11.45 p.m. (in George Yard) dead by **3.30 a.m.** discovered **4.50 a.m.** (George Yard buildings).

2. Polly Nichols, 31st August - Buck's Row (now Durward Street - the middle thereof) between **3.15 - 3.40 a.m.**

3. Annie Chapman, 8th September - Hanbury Street c. **5.30 a.m.**

4. Liz Stride, 30th September - Berner Street (now Henriques Street) **12.45 - 1.00 a.m.**

5. Catherine Eddowes, 30th September - Mitre Square **1.35 - 1.45 a.m.**

6. Mary Kelly, 9th November - Miller's Court, off Dorset Street. Last seen on the street, alive, at **2.00 a.m.** (cries of 'Murder!' heard around **4.00 a.m.**).

Either the killer was an East End resident, permanent or temporary, or he lived outside the immediate area. These and other data suggest he was, in fact, 'not among the ordinary denizens of the place' and that he stayed overnight when it met his purpose.

The Tabram, Nichols and Eddowes murders all have in common proximity to the Whitechapel Road, suggesting this thoroughfare was the killer's access route into the East End. However, events 1 and 2 are separated in time from the Eddowes killing by some two hours, whereas an hour (approx.) separates Stride from Eddowes. Self-evidently therefore Liz Stride's murder represented commencement of *that* night's foray, whereas 1, 2, 3 and 6 (Mary Kelly) are each nearer the conclusion of a night's visitation, with the culprit on his way home. But where *was* home? Obviously he was not to be seen at 13 Miller's Court following the butchery there.

The site in relation to victim no.2 is located to the East, across the Whitechapel Road from the London Hospital. Was the killer of Polly Nichols moving east or west along what was once Buck's Row? It is entirely possible that the anonymous stranger who told Patrick Mulshaw 'Watchman, old man, I believe someone is murdered down the street' was in fact responsible for Nichols' death. Indeed, his use of the phrase 'murdered' lends support to such conjecture. Notwithstanding the small group of people gathered where poor Polly lay, what led this passer-by to conclude she had in fact been murdered and not simply died of natural causes? It was dark and there was very little blood visible at the site.

This meeting with Mulshaw took place in Winthrop Street, a tributary positioned approximately mid-way along Buck's Row. It appears on maps as a dead-end to traffic, but there were no reports of the man doubling back, in the company of Mulshaw or otherwise. His indifference to either the prostrate figure on the pavement or, if he had arrived later on the scene, the inquisitive personnel also present, raises further suspicion.

Whilst Mulshaw proceeded to Buck's Row his informant quite possibly continued along the Winthrop Street footpath, eventually crossing the railway line at the station, stepping into the Whitechapel Road and continuing further east. (Pedestrian passageways were by no means uncommon in urban London at the time, even into the 1950s when the author was a child. They were typically bounded by large galvanized bollards – ideal for playing leapfrog!)

Once the killer's purpose was fulfilled on the night of September 30th, he again returned eastward, but neither directly along the Whitechapel Road, as one might expect, nor, being understandably furtive, along Old Montague Street, accessed via Commercial Street then Wentworth Street. Instead he turned north into Goulston Street. From there he might still have fled via Wentworth Street and beyond, but again, as we know, he did not. He moved onto Dorset Street (once infamous, now obliterated), where he washed his hands in a public hand-basin, then disappeared.

If the Whitechapel murderer's domicile lay to the east, as has been argued, why then did he not travel immediately in that direction after concluding his night's work on the 30th September? The answer lies in the timing. It was still very early in the morning. But why head north, and why Goulston Street? Because it projected eventually onto a junction with Dorset Street where there was an outside sink. Did the killer simply take advantage of this fortuitous circumstance? Only if for some reason he spontaneously decided to escape north rather than go east. Why should he have done that? Most probably because that would take him to an overnight lodging he had previously arranged and past a washing facility he already knew about.

Mary Kelly's killer too was happy to spend a few hours at 13 Miller's Court, having approached her along Commercial Street from the south, i.e., the Whitechapel Road end, at its junction with Thrawl Street.

Supposing a convenient 'stop-over' in the Dorset Street vicinity affords, surprisingly, a possible link to the location of the Nichols murder in Buck's Row, some distance away. We know the killer was familiar with Hanbury Street from the fact that Annie Chapman was murdered there. A straightforward 'left then second right' from Dorset Street would bring the pedestrian onto Hanbury Street. Pursuing this eastward to its conclusion, a 'right then left' would have led into Buck's Row (now Durward Street), moving away from the centre of Whitechapel, as the killer may well have done following Annie Chapman's murder.

The only anomaly, if such it be, is the murder of Elizabeth Stride in Berner Street (now Henriques Street), which is just off the Commercial Road, not the Whitechapel Road. However, these two arterial routes are linked at several points to the east of this fatal thoroughfare before they eventually converge. The Whitechapel murderer's meeting with Catherine Eddowes took place just west of this point of convergence, confirming that his direction of travel at the outset that night was east to west, whereas hours later it would be the reverse.

The reported encounter between shopkeeper's daughter Emily Marsh and an inquisitive stranger took place on premises at 218 Jubilee Street, Mile End Road (continuation of the Whitechapel Road). Jubilee Street lies, again, to the East of Whitechapel station/London Hospital and is divided at several points along its length. No. 218 is situated toward the head of the street, mid-way between Sidney Street and Stepney Green.

A corollary to these observations regarding the location of the Marsh trading post resides in the reason for the man's inquiry, i.e., the package postmarked that very day (15ᵗʰ October) and delivered the day following to George Lusk. The fellow could not have been carrying it in his hands, since he must have used both of them to write an approximation to Lusk's address (*sans* house number) in his note book. Perhaps he had it in his pocket all the while, the parcel being but three inches square. If not, then he would have had to return to wherever the kidney (or the package, if it were already prepared) was resident, simply in order to post it. How near or distant that residence may have been would naturally have had a bearing on when the consignment was despatched. George Lusk lived further to the east, Henry Statham further still.

As mentioned in chapter 1, Mary Jane Kelly was in the habit of affording temporary accommodation to others. Her temporary guests included a prostitute going by the name of Maria Harvey. The final straw for Jo Barnett though was 'when *Mr* Harvey came to stay'. One might reasonably suppose this individual was Maria's husband, but that is not necessarily the case. Furthermore, not knowing quite how this man and Barnett were introduced, one cannot specify whether the title 'Mr' was first employed by Mary Jane, or her paramour when giving evidence at her inquest. Taking this together with the fact that 'Harvey' can serve as either a surname or a Christian name raises the possibility that 'Jo' was introduced to 'Harvey' (and not as Mr Barnett). One might further speculate that Barnett could have misheard, or later misremembered, his partner's actual reference to 'Harry'. Were that to have been the case, it is worth bearing in mind that 'Harry' is as common a nickname for 'Henry' as it is an abbreviation of 'Harold'.

CHAPTER 17

THE INTERVENTIONIST

What, then, of Dr Henry Statham, collector of uterine instruments, who went from Paymaster to Instructor of Musketry, afterwards Ship's Doctor, eventually 'getting up evidence' on behalf of a London solicitor; evidence in connection with the case against Dr James Gloster in particular?

A comment attributed to Lord Cardigan (according to the script for the 1968 film, 'The Charge of the Light Brigade') epitomises the true level to which Henry Statham was elevated during the course of his military career:

> 'Officer', Paymaster Duberly? That ain't a rank,
> it's a trade.

One might also question the utility of obstetric devices to a doctor aboard a 19th c. naval vessel. Albeit part of a doctor's basic equipment, such 'tools of the trade' represent a very specific area of medical practice, one which may or may not have formed part of Dr Henry Statham's medical/surgical education. (Dr Gloster, it may be remembered, himself studied Obstetrics at a different place and time from his principal training in Medicine.)

For a *merchant ship's* doctor to offer obstetric services, he would obviously have to be aboard the ship in question. Yet there is no clear evidence of Statham's practising medicine aboard a ship of any description having arrived back in England. There can be little doubt, however, that any business correspondence Statham had with the Schummacher household will have had nothing whatever to do with ordering a dress!

Recalling the envelope produced in evidence before Magistrate d'Eyncourt at Ebury Bridge and addressed to Dr Henry Statham, by 'Miss Brady', whom Statham identified in court as a former employee of Eliza Schummacher's, how in fact might a lady, lately of Pimlico, have made the acquaintance of a lapsed doctor from Leighton with *investigative* business in the Strand, and why?

The second part of that question is the easier to answer and supports the suspicion that Dr Henry Statham, besides being a 'name' in 'Frisco', had a certain name among ladies of London besides. Furthermore, given the true, sordid context of the Schummacher case, what would be the chance likelihood of Eliza Schummacher and her former employee, Miss Brady, having written separately to one each of two individuals, who both then proceed to inject themselves into the *same* murder case, one way or another?

Statham lived at Leighton, Essex. His reported acquaintance, Robertson, lodged at Gower Street. They did not share an address. The court was not told by Statham exactly where this pair were at the time of their first exchange on the subject of the Gloster trial. And yet we apparently have these two ladies corresponding independently with one or other man.

*

Resigning the Queen's Commission as Ensign in 1860, Henry Statham saw service with the Indian Army (the military arm of the East India Company) nevertheless. He next spent a number of years in America, before returning to England in 1875. His 'alma mater' in the USA is unknown, but it is of interest to note that several erstwhile medical colleges located in Philadelphia, Pennsylvania, are recognized as having been illegal, fraudulent organizations, their alumni regarded as 'unregistered practitioners'. Statham considered himself to have something of a reputation on the eastern seaboard, and spoke colloquially of 'Frisco' when giving evidence in court;

evidence he signed off as truthful. (Did not the Met's detectives trail a doctor, believed to be from Pennsylvania, who was travelling under the name of Townsend?)

Surprisingly, the signature which Dr Henry Statham appended to his written statement for the magistrate is disturbingly similar to the handwriting on display within the Lusk letter. Observations on the part of Mr Nigel Moore, explain *how* similar:

> Without knowing the individual letters (no idea what the signature says), I would say the loops that exist are consistent with those appearing in the letter. The letter 'm', or possibly 'n', in the signature is also consistent with similar constructions in the letter. *Perhaps most striking is the formation of the letter 'y'. When it appears at the beginning of the word (see: 'you'), the loop turns to the left, as one would expect. However, when it appears at the end of the word (see: very, bloody and only) the loop turns sharply to the right, as if forming the tail to the letter 'q'. This trait is mirrored in the signature where the letter 'y' appears at the end of the first name.*
>
> I would also say the alignment and slant of the name, and the letters contained therein, is consistent with that appearing in the letter.

Whoever signed off the Lusk letter will, of course, have written it. Should one accept the Goulston Street graffito to have been the Whitechapel murderer's handiwork, then he must have written that too: written clues in tandem therefore, each with an Irish aspect, apparently.

Despite an obvious and immediate association with the recent death of Catherine Eddowes, the Lusk letter supports the belief that its author's murderous dealings extended both backwards and forwards in time from the date of the letter's receipt by George Lusk. 'I send you half the kidne I took from one woman', tells us immediately of other women from whom the killer did *not* extract a kidney, whilst, 'I may send you the bloody knif that took it out if you only wate a whil longer', informs the reader of a finale to come, following which he would hand over his knife. Of course we know what was acted out inside 13 Miller's Court. The author of (signatory to) that letter was the man police were desperate to apprehend, and who was confident he would evade them, hence: 'Catch me when you can, Mishter Lusk'.

The likely murderer was variously described, by those who caught a glimpse of him at least. Headgear in the form of a 'deerstalker's cap' is a feature that predominates. However, witness Joseph Lawende was able to furnish some additional detail:

> He wore a pepper-and-salt loose jacket, a grey
> cloth cap with a peak, and a reddish
> neckerchief tied in a knot.

Lawende thought he looked like a sailor.

Henry Statham, it should be recalled, had spent time at sea, as he explained:

> I don't know Dr Neville's address. He went to
> Darlington 3 or 4 weeks ago. He is, like
> myself, *a ship's doctor.* I mean, I used to be.

Lawende's mention of a 'reddish neckerchief' (worn by a sailor) has a certain resonance with George Hutchinson's mention of a red handkerchief being offered to Mary Kelly (by a gentleman).

Were this to have been the same man, and the same handkerchief, it would clearly lend credence to Hutchinson's account.

Not only is there a suggestion here that Kelly and her assailant *were* acquainted, but that, on this occasion, the individual deliberately dressed in a respectable manner, one more familiar to her than the workaday, 'scruffy genteel' image he conceivably adopted for his previous victims. At the time of his meeting with Kelly he was in fact very neatly dressed, sporting, as previously described, white spats to his shoes, an Astrakhan collar to his coat and a horse-shoe tie pin (a gentleman's accessory popular in the American West, don't forget). If this was to be the Whitechapel murderer's 'swan song', then maybe he was dressing for the occasion.

Very much nearer the time of the murders, another 'man about town' offered his own opinion as to the personage in whom the police, the press and the general public had an understandably keen interest.

On the night of the 7th August, Col. Sir Francis Charles Hughes-Hallett made his way to the George Yard site of Martha Tabram's murder - a Whitechapel homicide pre-dating that of Polly Nichols. He was afterwards quoted in the *Reno Evening Gazette* (8th October 1888, the story filed from New York City), as saying he had trailed a man soon after the 7th August murder:

> New York, October 6th. Colonel Hughes-Hallett of London, formerly of the Royal Artillery and a Member of Parliament, is in this city. He investigated the Whitechapel case just after the Martha Turner (*sic*) murder. He said today: 'I have made up my mind, and I have seen no reason to change it, that *the perpetrator of the atrocities is a West End man, a gentleman, a person of wealth and culture*

154

perhaps, but certainly of intellectual qualities, finesse, and keen discrimination. I was convinced that my man left his club as I was then doing, and disguised himself for his nocturnal revel. *My theory is that the Whitechapel murderer is an Army Doctor, or a medical student, or a gentleman, and a man of leisure. Or perhaps a retired Army Surgeon.'*

Various criminal profilers, including those of the FBI, have since offered their interpretations of the known evidence in the Whitechapel case, but there is one assessment which arguably carries most weight - that of police surgeon Dr Thomas Bond, who assisted in the autopsy of Mary Jane Kelly. Here is *his* profile of the scourge of Whitechapel:

> The murderer must have been a man of physical strength, and great coolness and daring. There is no evidence that he had an accomplice.

> *The murderer in appearance is quite likely to be a quiet inoffensive looking man, probably middle-aged, and neatly and respectably dressed.* I think he might be in the habit of wearing a cloak or overcoat, or could hardly have escaped notice in the streets if the blood on his hands or clothes were visible.

Mary Jane Kelly, it will be recalled, was last seen alive in the street, in the early hours, in the company of a man wearing a long coat trimmed with Astrakhan. He was also noticed by onlooker George Hutchinson to have been carrying a small parcel wrapped in American Cloth (a pre-cursor of PVC). A later need to remove blood from his hands would have been easily met, there being an outdoor sink nearby. Bond Continues:

> Assuming the murderer to be such a person as I have just described, he would be solitary and *eccentric in his habits,* also *he is likely to be a man without regular occupation, but with some small income or pension.* He is possibly living among respectable persons who have some knowledge of his character and habits and who may have grounds for suspicion that he is not quite right in his mind at times. Such persons would probably be unwilling to communicate suspicions to the Police for fear of trouble or notoriety, whereas if there were the prospect of reward it might overcome their scruples.

As regards the perpetrator's degree of surgical expertise, Dr Bond observed:

> In each case, the mutilation was inflicted by a person who had no scientific or anatomical knowledge. In my opinion he does not even possess the technical knowledge of a butcher or horse slaughterer, or any person accustomed to cutting up dead animals.

The surgical credentials of Dr Henry Statham are of course by no means established.

Dr Bond's profile of the Whitechapel murderer meshes neither comfortably nor completely with what is known of 34-year-old Dr James Gloster. On the other hand, it represents a surprisingly accurate description of Dr Henry Statham, a qualified surgeon (or so he claimed), who seems to have opted for premature retirement from the medical profession in favour of 'evidence gathering' and other business, but retained a small collection of obstetric devices nevertheless. Perhaps he had a point to prove.

Taken together, the opinions of Col. Hughes-Hallett and Dr Thomas Bond constitute a remarkable facsimile of this oddball individual:

A West End man, a gentleman

An Army Doctor, medical student or gentleman. A man of leisure. Perhaps a retired Army Surgeon

Probably middle-aged, neatly and respectably dressed, eccentric in his habits

A man without regular occupation, but with some small income or pension.

Henry Statham was an itinerant, professionally and domestically, whose American medical qualifications were questionable to say the least. A man of independent means, he had irregular 'business' with a Solicitor in the West End, near the Strand, but no regular occupation. Instead he enjoyed a modest pension!

At the time of the Gloster trial, Henry Statham had been resident at his Leighton address for fifteen months. Unlike Dr James Gloster he had no professional reason to frequent the Whitechapel district. Since he was not registered as a practising doctor, his services would not have been required by the London Hospital, for instance. Previously however, Dr Statham had likely resided at Blackthorn Street, affording him easier access both to Commercial Road and the Whitechapel Road, as well as acquaintance with the Whitechapel area.

Above all else there is the matter of motive to consider. Why should someone such as Henry Statham have suddenly gone on a killing spree, choosing a handful of down-and-out prostitutes as his victims? Although not exactly straightforward, the answer to that question is, I believe, to be found in the nature of the Schummacher case, and Statham's connection to it.

Henry Statham was a reluctant witness at the trial of Dr James Gloster, having been subpoenaed by Gloster's counsel to attend. He had previously visited the doctor's solicitor, as well as his Kensington practice, where he will have interacted with Thomas Gloster, who was 'holding the fort', so to speak, during his brother's travails. We have no idea what manner of conversation ensued between these men, or indeed between the latter and his brother's 'Silk', Mr Charles Gill, another Irishman. We have only Mr Gill's enigmatic observation to the court bench that he had 'intimated to his learned friend, as well as the Chief Clerk, Mr Safford, why he wished to call this man (Statham) as a witness, and felt it important the court heard what he had to say'.

In order to focus on Statham's position in all this, let us suppose that the defence camp were justified in claiming Dr James Gloster's innocence in the matter of Eliza Schummacher's untimely death. Might they not have brought forth Dr Gloster's sometime assistant, the neighbourly Dr Townsend, to refute the testimony of Eliza's sister, Emily Maud Baker? After all, it was she who claimed to have been instructed to refer her sister to the accused's West End associate, Dr Louis Tarrico, whom Dr Gloster himself had denied even knowing. One has to wonder quite why they chose *not* to call Dr Townsend as a witness for the defence.

Another aspect of Dr Gloster's presumed innocence would no doubt have been the team's reaction to Dr Henry Statham's arrival on the scene, together with his tale of a confession by *his own* associate, Dr Robertson, who was, sadly, unavailable for comment. This should have been seen as 'manna from heaven'. However, with Henry Statham as the only immediate source of reference regarding this extraordinary, and potentially exonerating third-party confession, it is altogether curious that several of the witnesses for the prosecution (i.e., 'employees' of Eliza Schummacher), were cross-examined as to whether they knew of, or recognized, *Henry Statham*, not whether they had seen or heard anything of a Dr Robertson.

From this one may reasonably infer that the gift Statham presented to the Gloster defence *was himself*, as a sacrificial lamb almost. Not quite what he had in mind perhaps, although he did announce in court that he'd be 'prepared to say *he* did it, if it would get the poor beggar (Gloster) off', presumably by causing a mistrial and 'immunising' the accused against being charged a second time should the spurious confession later be retracted. Nevertheless, he may well have felt that the attention of Mr Poland (prosecuting for the crown) was being unjustly diverted in his direction, and by an alliance of Irishmen into the bargain.

If Henry Statham should have formed that opinion, he would probably have reached an associated conclusion - that James Gloster was not the innocent party he claimed to be. His own acquaintance (Robertson) may perhaps have made an 'off the cuff' confession, but that could hardly be taken to guarantee he was actually guilty of the crime in question. If Gloster were indeed the true culprit, he will have known immediately that the Robertson confession was a fabrication. Hence it was Statham whom his defence counsel should attempt to manoeuvre into the role of suspect.

Henry Statham could conceivably have held something of a grudge against the Irish therefore, for having embroiled him unfavourably in defence of a possible murderer, however much he may have brought it upon himself in the first instance.

But would such brief interaction as Statham may have enjoyed with Thomas Gloster, while at the physician's Kensington practice, have been in any way sufficient to endow him with the subtleties of spoken Irish dialect? Would he have known, or even guessed, that the Glosters hailed from Limerick, where, in the colloquial language of the time, a sibilant (pronounced 'sh') would typically be substituted for a consonantal 't' in word-final position (e.g., 'oush of ish' for 'out of it'), whilst the county contributed its very name to a popular rhyming scheme? (The Lusk letter closed with 'Mishter Lusk'. The layout of the Goulston Street graffito appears, from Sir Charles Warren's transcription at least, to have vaguely resembled that of a 'limerick'.)

Surprisingly, Henry Statham's exposure to an Irish milieu quite possibly pre-dated the Whitechapel murders by a decade or more. Approximately half of all Irish immigrants to the State of Pennsylvania settled in and around Philadelphia, while the other half moved further west to the more rural areas, such as the county of Montgomery, where, positioned mid-way between Phoenixville and Pottstown, near a crooked bend in the Schuylkill River, is the township of *Limerick*.

Dr Henry Statham's student days in 'Philly' coincided exactly with trade union disputes in the Pennsylvania coalfields and the crescendo of criminal activity attributed at the time to the 'Molly Maguires'. The flames of that unrest were fanned by the 'great panic' (i.e., depression) of 1873, but were doused three years later by a series of murder trials, which saw all twenty accused hung for their crimes. In the midst of this turmoil, Statham left Pennsylvania for England (1875).

Intriguingly, the Molly Maguires, it is alleged (particularly by one Franklin B. Gowen), were in the habit of issuing their targets with what were described as 'coffin notices' – basically short announcements of impending doom for the recipient. (Gowen produced several examples at the 1876 trial of a number of 'Mollys'.)

It is tempting to view the Lusk letter in similar terms, both for the eventual sufferer and, albeit to a significantly lesser extent, the letter's addressee. Those written traces of the Molly Maguires that have come down to us display considerable variation in their degree of literacy, one or two revealing an erratic use of capital letters reminiscent of the Goulston Street graffito.

Ironically therefore, and despite this present line of inquiry being derived from it, the text of the Goulston Street graffito may have had no explicit connection with the Whitechapel murders beyond merely having been written by the culprit. It may have represented simply a conversational moment, recalled from over a decade past, and in a place where the Irish and Jewish communities were more conspicuously at loggerheads than Whitechapel even.

Whilst the Irish immigrant miners of Pennsylvania ran the risk of dying simply by doing their jobs, their industrialist employers, and by implication their financiers, were, then as now, primarily concerned to invest in efficiency, not safety. On the one hand mining disasters of the day were seen as preventable. On the other they were viewed as a commonplace nuisance interrupting the flow of profit.

Someone familiar at first hand with the Irish mode of thought and manner of expression gave vent to his own feelings on the streets of Whitechapel in 1888, perhaps cloaking his motive in a cryptic allusion to his own past, and a nationality to which he did not himself belong. In his book *Angela's Ashes*, an autobiographical account of life in Limerick (Ireland), Frank McCourt illustrates these expressive tendencies perfectly clearly:

> I'll sit next to you an' if there's one word out of the St. Vincent de Paul Society I'll take the face off 'em so I will.

And

> If 'tis a thing I ever find out you were telling jokes
> to Jesuits I'll tear the bloody kidney out of you.

The fate of Catherine Eddowes and that of Mary Jane Kelly spring immediately to mind.

However, we may appeal once again to the Goulston Street graffito in support of the contention that its author (and therefore the Whitechapel murderer) was neither Irish nor a Jew.

Leaving aside any peculiarly secretive (i.e., Masonic) interpretation of the word 'Juwes', and following Sir Charles Warren's premise that the writer was Irish, Jews his subject, we may reasonably ask the question: What possible relevance could reference to the Jews have had in the wake of an Irishman's having just killed a London streetwalker? And if the scribe were a Jew, intent on simply identifying with his compatriots, why adopt an Irish accent such as that 'heard' also in the Lusk letter? In any event a Jew would have been perfectly capable of identifying his people with three or four letters. He certainly would not have required five.

Thus the messenger quite possibly dressed himself in robes borrowed from his own previous experience, if not in South Kensington and the brief company of strangers, then conceivably several years spent in Pennsylvania, USA, re-enforced, perhaps, through his acquaintance with a young colleen at 13 Miller's Court, herself a native of Limerick, and who trusted her killer sufficiently to afford him overnight sanctuary once too often.

Being ready to confess to the murder of Eliza Schummacher when he had nothing whatsoever to do with her death is a measure of arrogance on Statham's part; an attitude perhaps fostered by the knowledge that he had *already* got clean away with similar misdeeds. His professional associations are also silently suggestive. Solicitor Maynard, who received his mail, and 'general enquiry officer' Hanson, who received £4 of his money, each did so in the Holborn district, a prestigious area within the City of London, where an American sporting a horseshoe tie pin, white spats and a long coat trimmed with Astrakhan would not have looked at all out of place. Certain it is that Henry Statham would not have been among the 'ordinary denizens' of Whitechapel.

For reasons already discussed, the unfortunate death of Eliza Schummacher, and the ensuing case against Dr James Gloster, may well have provoked the Whitechapel killer into an orgy of vengeance; a rampage that would characterize him forever as 'Jack the Ripper'.

EPILOGUE

My personal 'king in the car park' moment came a little over twenty years ago, when, following an intuition that something of significance had occurred to precipitate the Whitechapel murders, I searched for, and found, possibly relevant reportage printed in the London Times during the late spring/early summer of 1888. It was a second-order conjecture which proved to be correct. I knew nothing of the Gloster case previously and could not have guessed it would encompass surgical malpractice, prostitution, abortion, Ireland and America, as well as furnish a possible signatory to the Lusk letter.

A second revelation occurred with the much more recent BBC broadcast of Emilia Fox and Professor David Wilson's attempt to identify the perpetrator.

The peculiar distribution of dates with respect to the 'canonical five' struck me long ago as sufficient justification for exploring the potential significance of the number 39. That a HOLMES analysis should flag up a connection between the murder of Martha Tabram and those that followed has since validated the supposition.

Although the HOLMES finding of relevance was arrived at through an evaluation of criminal parameters entered into a relational database, if one takes the view, as I do, that the Whitechapel murderer was intent on making a statement of some kind, then the only aspect of the Tabram case which may obviously contribute to that interpretation is the number of wounds inflicted upon her, as the manner of her death differed entirely from that of the Ripper's other victims (it was reportedly achieved with different weaponry, i.e., a double-bladed knife of some kind, possibly a bayonet or dagger). With the notable exception of Mary Jane Kelly, who was attacked while indoors, the remainder of the 'canonical five' were first strangled then mutilated *post mortem.*

Considering the Tabram case as Jack the Ripper's handiwork was therefore a genuine prospect long before the BBC introduced Scotland Yard's digital Sherlock into the debate.

It was long ago speculated that with the death of Mary Jane Kelly the Whitechapel murderer reached a crescendo of fetishistic behaviour, after which he suffered a complete mental breakdown. A more prosaic explanation might be that Kelly suffered as she did simply for being Irish. Her death in the early hours of the 9th November 1888 coincided with the day of the Lord Mayor's parade. And yet there are other significant correspondences to be observed, particularly in connection with the veneration of certain individuals of classical antiquity.

The Catholic Church recognizes 'Four Crowned Martyrs' - Christian soldiers of ancient Rome, who were punished for refusing to offer a sacrifice to the image of Aesculapius, *god of medicine and healing.* This event is rumoured to have occurred during the reign of Diocletian, in the year a.d.307. The Quatuor Coronati of Masonic legend, on the other hand, were actually *five* stonemasons from Pannonia (since part of Austria-Hungary southwest of the Danube), whose martyrdom took place around two years earlier (a.d.305), after they had refused to fashion a statue of the same Aesculapius.

Five is precisely the number who met a symbolic end in London's Whitechapel in the autumn of 1888. Ironically, it was Liz Stride's death, not Martha Tabram's, which constituted the exception to the rule. Coincidentally, the feast date associated with four genuinely recorded martyrs, interred in Albano and cited in the Roman Calendar of Feasts, a.d.354, was the 7th August, the date of Martha Tabram's murder centuries later.

The question of whether the number 39 held a veiled significance for the Whitechapel murderer, as well as those for whom he left his scant clues, is fundamental here. Surprisingly, there is a historical precedent for just such communicative behaviour. More than two decades earlier another notable American saw fit to send a signal to his European audience, exploiting this very number.

Abraham Lincoln was not among those US presidents who were Freemasons, although he did apply to join the order before being elected. He went on to evince a number of its linguistic traits over time, but without ever actually becoming a member, apparently. It is nevertheless possible that he absorbed the principles of Freemasonry through a close personal friend, a Past Master Mason with the imaginative name of Bowling Green. Whatever the origin or extent of Lincoln's masonic understanding, the following series of events is on record as having taken place:

Authorities in Minnesota asked the President to order the immediate execution of 303 Indian males (Santee Sioux) found guilty of straying from their reservation in search of food, one band having stolen eggs from a white settler's land. Concerned with how this might be interpreted by the Europeans, whom he feared could yet enter the civil war on the side of the South, Lincoln offered the politicians of Minnesota a compromise: They would pare the list of those to be hung down to 39. In return, Lincoln promised to kill or remove every Indian from the state and provide Minnesota with 2 million dollars in federal funds. (He owed the Sioux only $1.4 million for their land.)

Although some commentators since have referred to the execution of 38 individuals, the actual number involved is beyond doubt, as all 39 were explicitly identified by name and prisoner number in a letter from the president to Brigadier General H. H. Sibley dated 6th December, 1862.

39 is neither a rounded fraction nor exact percentage of 303. What factor determined this guilty sub-set therefore? Whatever the number 39 signified for Lincoln, this episode clearly lends weight to the contention that the Whitechapel murderer too endeavoured to communicate with Europeans via the very same numeral, and an appeal to the calendar. In short, he announced both his affiliation and his intention on the 7th August, thereafter proceeding to complete a symbolic paradigm of martyrdom. His victims were sacrificial representatives of their kind, another member of which had been responsible for his coming to public attention as a potential murderer. Acting as he did ensured he would 'not be blamed for nothing'.

As regards who, exactly, might have done the acting, consider the Dubliner, Tennant; the tenant who may conceivably have written that prescient letter from 22 Hammersmith Road. It is not at all improbable that this gentleman followed the news of both the Whitechapel murders *and* the case involving his near neighbour, Dr Gloster. Might he have 'put two and two together' perhaps? If so, Gloster's third-party connections with Clapham and the West End might well have been those referred to in that very letter, concluding with an Italianate reference to 'Lunigi' into the bargain.

But what about the predicted date, 9th November? However alert said author may have been to local gossip, killers are not known to announce the specific date of their future crimes. The possibility exists therefore that the anonymous correspondent spotted the all-important numerical correlation, and simply prophesied the inevitable, 9th November.

The significance of this letter thus resides, neither in the surprisingly accurate prediction as to timing, nor its seemingly inaccurate predictions of place, but in its unification of characteristics pertinent to two ostensibly unrelated cases, that of

Regina vs. Gloster and the unsolved Whitechapel Murders, drawn together, as like as not, by an Irishman.

The 1988 centenary edition of the BBC's Timewatch programme, 'Shadow of the Ripper' featured writer Christopher Frayling, who interviewed a number of participants besides. Among them was Dr Murray Cox, then Consultant Psychotherapist at Broadmoor Hospital, who made a rather telling observation:

> I think it would be generalizable to say that it is highly likely that somewhere deep inside Jack the Ripper there would be something to do with regulation of self-esteem, either the recovery of lost self-esteem or an attempt to establish self-esteem which he never had.

Surely this assessment is reflected in the words, "the Juwes are the men who will not be blamed for nothing." Intriguingly, a light-hearted computer analysis of Henry Statham's signature, undertaken years ago, interpreted the signature's author as being, among other things, 'over concerned with the cost of their actions'.

A gentleman's appearance in a court of law, whether as the accused or as a witness under subpoena and unusually close scrutiny, whose evidence is dismissed out of hand, is indeed likely to engender a loss of self-esteem. If this, or a similar circumstance, were viewed as an affront by the eventual Whitechapel murderer, his subsequent victims will have articulated his retort.